SAFETY

for the

HVACR Service Technician

The HVACR Training Authority

Cover photos reprinted with permission. Top right: SPX CORPORATION. Bottom left: FLUKE CORPORATION.

ISBN-13: 978-1-61607-133-2
ISBN-10: 1-61607-133-8

TABLE OF CONTENTS

▶ **FOREWORD** ◀

The purpose of this book is to provide a single source for the many various safety materials that RSES has developed specifically for the HVACR service technician. The information presented in this publication includes numerous safety facts, guidelines, and recommendations. However, the suggestions made are, for the most part, general in their meaning and may not be applicable to all situations or conditions.

Remember: "Safety Is Job One" is more than a slogan—it's an everyday work practice that must be kept in mind and followed by everyone from the owner of the business all the way down to the newest apprentice on the job. Accidents on the job site can result in injury, death, and considerable expense in the form of lost time, property damage, medical costs—and, in some instances, large fines for the business owner. Employers must ensure that a safety program is in place and that every employee receives safety training. For all of these reasons, technicians employed in the HVACR industry must observe proper safety precautions in order to protect themselves, their fellow workers, their customers, and others who may be occupying the job site.

Introduction to Safety

INTRODUCTION

Technicians who install, maintain, and service heating, cooling, ventilation, and refrigeration equipment have a great responsibility when it comes to observing safe working practices on the job. They must be thoroughly familiar with all of the following aspects of safety:

- ▶ personal safety
- ▶ occupant and user safety
- ▶ equipment function safety
- ▶ compliance with government (federal, state, and local) safety regulations.

PERSONAL SAFETY

Anyone entering a mechanical trade must always be taught to give safety the highest priority. As an HVACR service technician, you can be exposed to many hazards. At no time can you "let down your guard." You must *always* be alert to potential safety hazards.

The list of job-related dangers is a long one. If you work on electrical components, for example, you must guard against electric shock. If you service oil heating equipment, burns are a risk. If you service gas heating equipment, you must be alert to possible ignition and combustion problems. Soldering and brazing present obvious fire hazards. Handling refrigerants requires an awareness of toxicity levels. Steam erupting from leaks or blow-off from safety valves can be extremely dangerous. Hydraulic pressure buildup from the expansion of heated water in a closed system can have disastrous results. These are just a few examples of the many personal safety hazards that you may encounter as an HVACR service technician.

Some job sites present other health hazards—hazards that may not be equipment-related and may vary from region to region throughout the country. For example, bites from insects, snakes, rats, and other animals can lead to badly infected wounds or diseases, such as rabies. Cuts and abrasions can become infected, and parasitic infections may, on occasion, be a serious problem. Bacteria also may infect cuts and abrasions, leading to the need for medical treatment, even though the original wound did not require first aid. General protective measures should be implemented to control such problems.

Always think "safety first" while working on any type of equipment in any type of environment. Avoid taking chances. By following safe work practices, you will protect yourself and others in the vicinity.

OCCUPANT AND USER SAFETY

As a service technician, one of your most important responsibilities is to the occupants and users of the conditioned premises. Faulty equipment can lead to tragic results, as can technician errors. Undetected gas leaks can cause harmful explosions, as can relief valves that are not working properly. Improper venting can result in carbon monoxide poisoning of the atmosphere. These types of accidents happen all too frequently.

The service technician is responsible for testing safety devices, such as safety valves, to ensure that they are not blocked or improperly adjusted. You should test high-temperature limit controls, high-pressure safety controls, and other safety controls on a regular basis. Gas-fired heat exchangers also should be tested regularly to assure occupants of safe performance.

Carefully check all electrical wiring when you install or service equipment. Improperly insulated conductors should be repaired or replaced promptly. Fires frequently start due to overheated equipment if high-temperature safety limit devices have been improperly adjusted or have failed due to age. The need for proper calibration or replacement of such devices is imperative.

Most important of all, you must *never* bypass, shunt out, or otherwise eliminate any defective or inoperative safety device, and *never* allow equipment to continue to operate without such devices. Such actions endanger not only your own safety, but also that of other occupants of the area.

EQUIPMENT FUNCTION SAFETY

The equipment that you service is often expensive. It is your responsibility to ensure that no damage is caused by the lack or misapplication of safety controls. Manufacturers generally issue instructions for installing and adjusting equipment to ensure proper operation. Equipment should *never* be used for any purpose other than that for which it is designed. If necessary, the service technician must go against the owner's desire to misapply or misuse equipment. Damage to the equipment ultimately reflects on the technician's performance and may lead to costly lawsuits, especially when it results in injuries.

COMPLIANCE WITH FEDERAL, STATE, AND LOCAL REGULATIONS

Before any equipment is installed, installers must observe local regulations regarding permits required for the installation. They must provide assurance that the installation will comply with the appropriate codes. Installers must be sure that equipment, once installed, is operating safely. It cannot at any time endanger the lives of the owner or occupants.

The national code covering safety is called the Occupational Safety and Health Act (OSHA). Issued by the federal government, this code covers in great detail the safety requirements for equipment. It also covers personal safety of installers and service technicians. It is a large legal document, but service technicians must be familiar with at least those parts of the law that apply to their trade. It is highly recommended that service technicians read carefully all publications and bulletins that describe the requirements with which they must comply.

In order to be sure that safe practices for installation and application are followed, technicians must also follow all manufacturers' instructions when installing the equipment. Normally, these instruction documents must be present when inspections are completed by the local code inspection officials to ensure that the equipment is installed according to the manufacturer's recommendations.

The National Fire Protection Association (NFPA) periodically publishes revisions of the U.S. National Electrical Code (NEC). The Canadian Standards Association (CSA) also regularly updates its requirements. Electrical equipment and wiring must comply with all applicable codes. If it does not, it will not be accepted by the insurance underwriters. In addition to compliance with U.S. and Canadian codes, most insurance underwriters require electrical equipment to carry an Underwriters Laboratories (UL) label or, in Canada, similar evidence of acceptance by the CSA.

Local government bodies also enact safety codes that installers must know, and comply with, during equipment installation. Technicians should acquaint themselves with, or have available, the appropriate codes that apply for their local areas. These codes are evidence of the importance attached to the matter of safety both by insurance companies and by government bodies. It is too late to consider safety when a fire occurs, or when a serious accident befalls the owner of the equipment that you have installed. It is much better to check all safety rules and requirements and abide by them when installing, maintaining, and servicing the system.

Despite all of these efforts, the record of accidents in the heating, air conditioning, and refrigeration industry is too high. While it is probably true that no other industry presents a greater variety of possible hazards to those involved in it, these hazards *can* be avoided. Greater effort must be placed on recognizing their sources and causes.

OSHA, your employer, and your fellow workers all have a part in creating a safe work environment. But remember: *The ultimate responsibility for safety on the job belongs to you!* ■

Types of Accidents

ACCIDENTS—THEIR CAUSES AND NATURE

The HVACR service technician is exposed to a number of hazardous conditions on the job. Most accidents can be avoided, and certainly they can be avoided more effectively if you are aware of their sources. Injuries in the HVACR industry can be divided into six general classifications, according to the cause and nature of the injury. They are:

▶ injuries resulting from mechanical malfunction or human error
▶ injuries resulting from electrical causes
▶ injuries resulting from excessively high pressures
▶ burns and scalds
▶ injuries resulting from explosions
▶ injuries resulting from the inhalation of toxic and non-toxic gases.

INJURIES RESULTING FROM MECHANICAL CAUSES

These types of injuries originate from working around moving machinery and from handling heavy loads. They also include injuries resulting from falls and from the improper use of tools. They constitute the largest percentage of accidents in the HVACR industry. In this category are:

▶ broken arms, legs, and other serious accidents that result from being caught in moving machinery or from having clothes, gloves, jewelry, etc. entangled in machinery
▶ injuries caused by objects and parts dislodged and thrown at high speed from moving machinery
▶ smashed fingers, toes, hands, or feet (from being hit with hammers or from having heavy objects dropped on them)
▶ falls from ladders or on slippery floors
▶ eye injuries and cuts and lacerations of the skin (due to slipping screwdrivers, saws, drills, or other edged tools).

Some protection from these types of accidents can be provided by guards on the machines, automatic trip switches, and other mechanical and electrical protective devices. But the best safeguard is the constant vigilance of the technician.

ELECTRICAL INJURIES

Most HVACR equipment is electrically driven, and the systems use electric control circuits. A thorough knowledge of how to work on and around this equipment safely is absolutely vital to the service technician. There are three general types of hazards directly associated with electricity:

▶ **Electric shock.** A person can be affected by an extremely small amount of electric current. It can take as little as 5 mA (five thousandths of an ampere) to cause the inability to let go (see Table 1).

▶ **Burns.** Burns are caused by direct contact with electric current, and a severe burn can be received from an electric arc. An arc can be caused by a bad switch or a broken wire. Electrical burns are painful and slow to heal.

▶ **Blast.** The pressure wave resulting from the intense, sudden heating of material in the path of an electric arc, and from the air immediately surrounding it, can be very powerful.

▼ **Table 1** Causes and effects of electric shock

Current (in milliamperes*)	Effect on the human body
Less than 0.5 mA	No sensation
2 to 10 mA	Muscles contract
5 to 25 mA	Painful shock, inability to let go
Over 25 mA	Violent muscle contractions
50 to 100 mA	Heart convulsions (ventricular fibrillation), possible death
Over 100 mA	Heart paralysis, inability to breathe, burns, almost certain death
*1 mA = 0.001 A	

Related accidents are a "consequential" hazard associated with electricity. A mild shock may not be severe enough in itself to injure you, for example. But what if the shock causes you to lose your balance and fall from a ladder? A fall can cause serious injury, permanent disability, or death. The person who receives a shock instinctively pulls away—possibly stepping off a scaffold, into moving machinery, or into open electric switches, live parts, or hot wires.

INJURIES RESULTING FROM HIGH PRESSURES

A basic characteristic of mechanical refrigeration is the use of various fluids—both gases and liquids—at pressures above atmospheric pressure. They must therefore be contained and transported in tanks, pipes, and other vessels that are constructed in such a way that they will not allow the fluids to leak. These components must be strong enough to withstand maximum pressures, under extreme operating conditions, without splitting or bursting.

Another basic characteristic of mechanical refrigeration is that pressures change with changes in temperature, or are increased by compressors or pumps. The service technician must therefore guard against extra pressures caused by compressors and pumps, as well as the pressures existing in the system because of variations of temperature.

Pressure-containing vessels and tubes are designed and constructed to withstand "normal" pressures—those caused by normal temperatures, normal degrees of compression, and normal filling of the vessels. If the vessel or tube is overheated, overpressurized, or overfilled, the vessel may "give" somewhat. When it reaches its limit of elasticity, however, the vessel will burst—often with explosive violence.

Excessive pressures may cause large parts, such as the soldered ends of driers or receivers, to be blown out. Overpressure also may drive plugs or other small parts out with projectile speed. If a cylinder or any other vessel shows a bulge, however small, relieve the pressure *immediately*. It may burst at any moment.

BURNS AND SCALDS

The risk of being burned is one that HVACR service technicians must take very seriously. Fire hazards include flammable refrigerants, gases, solvents, and fuel oils. When working with or near sources of ignition—burners, soldering torches, etc.—you must exercise extreme caution. (Chapter 11 contains a more thorough discussion of fire safety.) Fire is not the only danger, however. You can also be burned or scalded by steam, hot water, and hot oil. Touching hot pipes or other uninsulated parts can result in burns and blisters to exposed skin. Contact with refrigerants and acidic mixtures of refrigerant and oil can cause chemical burns.

INJURIES RESULTING FROM EXPLOSIONS

Explosion and flammability are so closely related that almost everything said about flammability applies equally well to explosion. If a flammable vapor ignites in an open space, it burns. In burning, it endangers not only the surrounding premises, but also the occupants and the service technician. If the vapor is confined—or worse, compressed and then ignited—it seeks more room, so it pushes outward with tremendous force and explodes, or causes an "explosion." The only practical difference between a gas catching fire and a gas exploding is that with the explosion there is violence and physical damage as well as flames.

INJURIES CAUSED BY TOXIC GASES

The word "toxic" means "poisonous," so *toxicity* is the condition of being poisonous. Refrigerants and other gases vary a great deal in their degrees of toxicity. The harmful effects depend on the nature of the gas itself, its concentration in the air, and the length of time it is breathed.

Some gases, such as ammonia and sulfur dioxide, are so highly toxic that it is dangerous as well as unpleasant to breathe air that contains only a few parts of the gas in a million parts of the air. Others may be inhaled in larger percentages when mixed with air, or for longer periods of time, before they become dangerous. It must be remembered, however, that the gas "Mother Nature" intended us to breathe is air. Any other gas is harmful. The harmful effects of a gas depend on:
- the nature of the gas itself
- its concentration in air
- how long a time it is breathed.

OTHER ACCIDENT SOURCES
Radiation

Radiographic machines that generate x-rays or utilize radioactive materials as a source of gamma or other radiation produce *ionizing* radiation. These types of machines are used for evaluating welds, pipes, joints, etc. Lasers used for aligning pipes produce very intense *non-ionizing* radiation. Welding produces ultraviolet light, which is hazardous to the eyes and skin. If proper safeguards are not observed, both ionizing and non-ionizing radiation can be very dangerous. Only qualified and trained personnel should be assigned to use such equipment.

Heat and cold

Provisions should be made to keep personal temperature within normal limits when you are exposed to extreme heat and cold. The obvious dangers include heat stroke, hypothermia, and frostbite, but exposures to heat and cold also can result in fatigue, discomfort, job inefficiency, sunburn, collapse, and other health problems (see sidebars previous page and this page).

REPORTING ACCIDENTS

All accidents, regardless of severity, must be reported without delay. In the event of an accident, the following important steps should be taken to ensure a prompt and proper investigation:

SAFETY TIP

Working in cold weather poses health dangers

Hypothermia results from the loss of body temperature and can occur even when temperatures are above freezing. Symptoms include shivering, loss of consciousness, and decreasing pulse and breathing rates. If a worker shows these symptoms, immediately call emergency medical services, move the person to a warm area, and warm the body slowly. Do not give the person food or drink. To prevent hypothermia, eat nourishing foods and dress in layers. Dress to prevent heat from escaping from head, underarm, and groin areas.

Frostbite results from ice crystals forming on body tissue, especially on the ears, nose, chin, fingers, and toes. The temperature must be below freezing for frostbite to occur. Symptoms include flushed skin, then white or grayish yellow skin, then grayish blue skin. If a worker shows signs of frostbite, immediately move the person to a warm area, place the frozen body part in warm (not hot) water, and quickly call a health care provider. To prevent frostbite, cover ears, nose, cheeks, chin, fingers, and toes with warm clothing, and immediately move to a warm area as soon as a body part begins to hurt.

SOURCE: MCAA REPORTER

▶ Report all accidents to your employer and/or supervisor *immediately*.

▶ A complete record of the accident should be kept by the employer and/or supervisor at the job site.

▶ Current codes and regulations should be reviewed for specifications relating to the accident.

▶ For serious accidents, the accident site must be left intact and undisturbed until all investigations are completed. Never move any equipment or tools involved in the accident until authorized to do so. ■

Job Site Safety

All individuals involved in the service or installation of HVACR equipment have a responsibility to practice safety at all times. This Chapter provides a general overview of some of the important factors that contribute to safety on the job site. Who is responsible for safety in the workplace? *Everyone!* This includes the contractor, the employer, the supervisors, and the workers. As an HVACR technician, it is usually in your own hands to make sure that your working environment is safe. Some larger job sites may have an on-site safety manager, but that does not override the responsibilities of all individuals on the job site.

The *contractor* (the person who undertakes a job for an owner and works in conjunction with the owner) must ensure that:

▶ the measures and procedures required by current OSHA (Occupational Safety and Health Administration) regulations are provided for and met on the job site
▶ employers and workers on the job site comply with these regulations
▶ the health and safety of workers on the job site are protected.

The *employer* must ensure that:

▶ the equipment, materials, and protective equipment required by law are provided
▶ the equipment, materials, and protective equipment are maintained in good condition and are used as prescribed
▶ all measures and procedures required by law are carried out
▶ information, instruction, and supervision are provided to protect the health and safety of all workers
▶ a competent person is appointed as supervisor.

The *supervisor* must ensure that:
▶ workers are advised of any potential or actual dangers to their health or safety
▶ workers are provided with instructions regarding the measures and procedures to follow for their protection, and that they observe all such measures and procedures
▶ workers use the personal protective equipment, devices, and clothing required by the employer.

The *worker* must:
▶ work in compliance with all rules and regulations
▶ use the personal protective equipment, devices, and clothing required by the employer
▶ report to the employer or supervisor any problem with the equipment or any hazard on the job site that may endanger workers or others
▶ report to the employer or supervisor any violation of the job site rules and regulations
▶ *never* work in a manner that may endanger anyone
▶ *never* engage in any prank, contest, feat of strength, unnecessary running, or rough and boisterous conduct on the job site (*no horseplay!*)
▶ report all accidents immediately to the employer or supervisor.

INSTRUCTIONS FOR NEW WORKERS

All new workers on a job site must receive instructions regarding personal safety. This means that you should be informed about where the first aid station, fire extinguishers, exits, and restrooms are located. You should be made aware of any possible work hazards and emergency procedures, and be introduced to the health and safety representative on the project, before you begin work. If you're new to a job site and don't receive this information, ask your supervisor.

HOUSEKEEPING

"Housekeeping" is a way of practicing preventive maintenance and helping to ensure that the possibility for accidents is minimized. Clean-up, disposal, and the proper storage of materials and equipment are essential for fire prevention and personal protection for all people on the job. Here are a few suggestions to aid in housekeeping:
▶ Materials must be stored in a manner that prevents tipping, falling, or collapsing.
▶ To prevent accidents, the disposal of waste and debris from overhead should be done by manually carrying trash down stairs, lowering it in containers, or using a disposal chute.

▶ **SAFETY TIP** ◀

Drive defensively to reduce accidents

Getting to the job site on a timely basis is one of the fundamental services you provide. But what if there's an accident en route?

Many of the vehicle insurance claims filed every year involve rear-end collisions, an accident that can easily be prevented with just a few simple precautions.

First, all drivers need to understand that there's no such thing as "stopping on a dime." The stopping distance (total distance needed to come to a complete stop) of a car traveling at 60 mph on hard, dry pavement is 366 ft (112 m), longer than the length of a football field!

Larger vehicles take even more space to stop. A pickup truck or a heavy two-axle truck needs 436 ft (133 m), and a three-axle truck needs up to 531 ft (162 m). If the pavement is wet, the road is sloped downhill, or the brakes are poorly adjusted, the distance can increase significantly.

To reduce the risk of rear-end collisions, follow these three tips:
▷ Look beyond the vehicle in front of you when driving on a straight-away. This will help you stay alert to changing conditions and can provide those vital extra seconds

(continued next page)

▶ Materials that require a crane or similar lifting device should not be stored under or near overhead power lines.

▶ All work and traffic areas should be kept clear of materials, equipment, and tools that are not in use.

▶ All work and traffic areas must be well lit. Missing or burned-out bulbs should be replaced as soon as possible.

▶ Fire extinguishers (of the proper type) must be readily available, regularly inspected and maintained, and refilled as soon as possible after use.

PERSONAL PROTECTIVE EQUIPMENT

Part of being safe on the job is wearing the proper clothing and using those items classified as *personal protective equipment* (PPE). No HVACR technician should arrive at the job site without proper eye protection, for example, whether it takes the form of goggles, face shields, or safety glasses with side shields. *Always* wear splash-protective goggles or a face shield when working with dangerous fluids, and when working with or handling refrigerants. Gloves, hard hats, and ear plugs are among the other items that fall into the category of PPE, which is discussed in greater detail in Chapter 4.

SERVICE VEHICLES

Service technicians should always observe proper safety practices in and around their service vehicles. Simple guidelines include:

▶ Follow commonsense rules of good driving (see sidebars) and keep service vehicles in good repair.

▶ Before you drive, make sure that equipment and materials are evenly distributed in the vehicle.

▶ Secure any and all cargo that could shift during travel, especially cylinders of compressed gas that must be kept in an upright position (see Figure 1 on the next page).

▶ Keep the vehicle clean inside and outside. Do not let debris and trash accumulate in the vehicle. Clean it regularly.

▶ Be careful when backing up, especially in cramped or congested areas. Do not back up without assistance—there is a blind area behind most vans and trucks.

▶ Make a habit of always walking around your vehicle before starting and moving it to make sure that the area is clear of obstructions.

▶ *Always* wear your seat belt.

MATERIAL SAFETY DATA SHEETS

A *material data safety sheet* (MSDS) should be available on the job site for each material and product that is being used. In addition, each service

---

(continued from previous page)

needed to come to a stop safely. Being conscious of traffic conditions ahead gives you the opportunity to predict and avoid possible accident situations.

▷ Keep a safe interval between your vehicle and the one ahead by using the three-second rule As the vehicle ahead passes a fixed point, such as a bridge or lamp post, begin counting: one thousand one, one thousand two, one thousand three. If you reach the fixed point before you finish counting, you're too close to the vehicle in front to make a safe stop. Remember, this rule applies to ideal road and weather conditions. Rain, ice, snow, or reduced visibility will require greater following distance.

▷ Use directional signals every time you turn or change lanes. Even this small change in habit can make a big difference in the number or possibility of accidents. Accidents involving lane changes are among the most severe, so proper use of turn signals can result in a substantial reduction of damage and injury.

By keeping a proper interval, you not only can reduce accidents and injuries, you can improve your public relations. Remember, your company's name is on the vehicle. If you tend to tailgate, slow down and back off.

SOURCE: ACCA

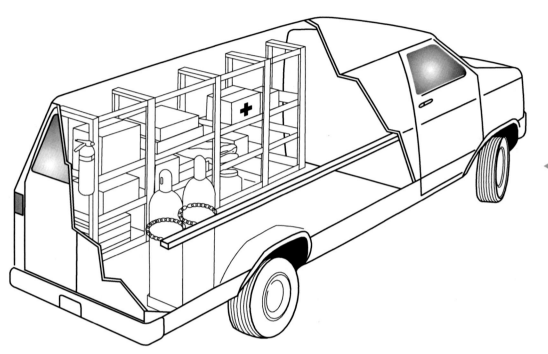

◀ **Figure 1** *Service truck with properly secured cargo*

vehicle should have on board a binder containing the MSDSs for all materials carried in the vehicle. An MSDS must provide:

- ▶ product information
- ▶ hazardous ingredients
- ▶ physical data
- ▶ fire and explosion data
- ▶ reactivity data
- ▶ information on health effects
- ▶ preventive measures
- ▶ first aid measures
- ▶ the name and phone number of the party preparing the MSDS and the date of preparation.

HAZARDOUS ENVIRONMENTS

Some job locations can be more hazardous than others because of the presence of certain materials or substances in the area. The following paragraphs identify a few of these potentially more hazardous situations.

Fire hazards

Fire hazards associated with working on HVACR equipment may be classified under several chief sources, including refrigerants, solvents, fuels, construction materials, and the refrigerated products themselves. The service technician or installer also must be aware of the highly flammable gases used in welding, soldering, and brazing operations—often in close proximity to other flammable materials. These conditions pose an ever-present threat to property and human life by fire or explosion. For more information on fire safety, see Chapter 11.

Gas-filled rooms

Rooms that contain flammable gases are potential bombs. They can be set off with a match, a lighted cigarette, a spark from an electric switch, or static electricity. Be especially careful in rooms containing gases from a flammable refrigerant or fumes from gasoline, naphtha, or other flammable solvents or fluids. Make sure all areas are well-ventilated.

Laboratories and surgical or anesthetizing rooms in hospitals and other medical facilities can contain ether or other anesthetic gases that can be flammable or explosive. Never install equipment with open-type motors or switches that may arc (such as window units or ventilating fans) in these locations. Use specially enclosed explosion-proof motors, switches, and relays. Avoid the use of drill motors, heat guns, or other hand tools that may create sparks or electric arcs. Remember that even static electricity sparks are dangerous in such rooms.

Handling refrigerant cylinders

Refrigerant cylinders are designed and constructed for definite maximum pressures and quantities of refrigerant based on specified maximum temperatures (usually 125°F, or 52°C). When cylinders are overfilled or improperly stored at temperatures above the stated specifications, the liquid expands, resulting in extremely high hydrostatic pressures. When this happens, refrigerant is vented into the space, displacing the breathable air. If the cylinder's relief device does not vent properly, the cylinder may burst, releasing the contents and projecting pieces of the metal canister outward with tremendous force.

Working with acids, caustic liquids, and alkaline cleaners

When working with any chemical solution (e.g., using hydrochloric acid to clean a condenser coil), wear approved goggles and gloves. Avoid breathing the fumes or spilling the chemical solution. In the event of skin contact, wash with water, then with water containing baking soda. For eye contact, flush with water for at least 15 minutes and get medical attention.

Always handle chemical solutions of any type with care. Containers must be labeled, kept tightly closed, and vented periodically to relieve internal pressure, particularly in hot weather. Keep containers away from heat and ignition sources. Never reuse containers for other purposes. Even washed containers retain residues and should be disposed of as hazardous waste.

 WARNING: When preparing a chemical solution, *always add the chemical to the water.* Adding the water to the chemical can make the solution boil up and splash you.

Working in confined spaces

One of the biggest dangers of working in a confined space is the failure to recognize that a confined space *is* a potential hazard (see sidebar). A confined space is not only a cramped area in which *your* movement is restricted, but one in which the natural movement of air is restricted. The lack of air flow means that the threat of explosion, poisoning, or asphyxiation is present. If the space contains equipment with moving parts, the danger is increased.

Hazardous atmospheres encountered in confined spaces fall into four distinct categories:
- flammable
- toxic
- irritant and/or corrosive
- asphyxiating.

A *flammable* condition generally occurs when combustible gases (acetylene, butane, propane, hydrogen, methane, etc.) or vapors become trapped in a confined space with inadequate ventilation. Welding, brazing, or soldering in a confined space is dangerous and is one of the major causes of explosions.

Substances regarded as *toxic* cover a wide spectrum of gases, vapors, and finely divided airborne dust. Toxic atmospheres may result from manufacturing processes, from operations performed in confined spaces (e.g., welding or brazing with metals capable of producing toxic fumes), and from products being stored. Carbon monoxide (CO) is a good example of a common hazardous gas that can build up in a confined space. It is odorless and colorless, and requires a specific test for detection. Carbon monoxide poisoning is not limited to any particular industry (see sidebar, next page).

Examples of *irritants* include chlorine, ozone, hydrochloric acid, hydrofluoric acid, sulfuric acid, nitrogen dioxide, ammonia, sulfur dioxide, benzene, carbon tetrachloride, and ethyl chloride. Irritant and corrosive atmospheres can be found not only in the HVACR industry, but also in plastics plants, chemical plants, the petroleum industry, paint manufacturing, and mining operations. Exposure to irritant or corrosive concentrations in a confined space may not be apparent immediately, but can occur over time and may result in a general weakening of the defense reflexes.

The danger of being *asphyxiated* (to be deprived of air) or made severely ill from breathing a toxic gas is more apt to occur if the gas has little or no odor. Individuals may breathe enough of these types of gases to be harmful over time, but may not realize that the gas is toxic until it is too late.

Ammonia and sulfur dioxide gases are very powerful. They immediately attack the eyes, throat, and mucous membranes, producing such painful effects that people exposed to them attempt to get away from the gas as quickly as possible. The eyes, throat, and lungs can be burned severely by ammonia and sulfur dioxide, especially if a person does not have sufficient warning and cannot get out of the area before being overcome.

Some gases can be dangerous in a short period of time if the percentage of the gas in the air is very high. If the percentage of the gas in the air is small, the air can be breathed for a much longer time, but the end result is still deadly. That is, the effect of these gases is *cumulative*—the effects keep building up, until finally the human system, especially the liver and kidneys, become so affected that the person eventually becomes very sick.

Artificial or natural gas used in cooking, heating, and water heating has a distinctive odorant added. If you can detect such an odor, ventilate the room before you attempt to work in it. If the odor is strong, be careful about going into the room even to open a window. A supplied-air respirator may be required for entering the space. A cloth over the mouth or nose, wet or dry, is *not* a gas mask—although many people have died thinking that it was. No one is immune to asphyxiation. Take no chances. Always be alert!

Victims overcome by gas first feel drowsy, and perhaps sick to the stomach. Or, if the concentration of gas is a heavy one, they become weak, the knees give way, and they find that although conscious, they cannot walk or crawl. Unconsciousness and death may follow.

Asphyxiating conditions occur when a significant amount of oxygen in a confined space is consumed or displaced. The *consumption* of oxygen can take place during the combustion of flammable substances (e.g., welding, heating, cutting, brazing). The number of people working in a confined space and the extent of their physical activity also can influence the oxygen consumption rate. The *displacement* of oxygen by other nontoxic inert gases (nitrogen,

---

▶ **SAFETY TIP** ◀

Saving lives with CO checks

HVAC contractors and technicians can be the first line of defense in protecting homeowners and businesses from carbon monoxide (CO) poisoning. It is believed that 5,000 people are treated each year in the U.S. for CO poisoning, with at least 300 deaths annually.

What can you do to protect customers?
▷ Notify customers of the importance of having their heating systems checked every year.
▷ Offer service agreement deals designed to promote heating equipment checks, and to examine any CO leaks.
▷ Recommend that your customers purchase CO monitors and detectors.
▷ Carry CO detectors/monitors in your service vehicle so that you can sell and install them.
▷ Check all appliances for any possible CO leaks.
▷ Explain to customers how to respond to a CO alarm.
▷ Make sure that the space is adequately ventilated.
▷ Check the chimney annually. A clogged chimney can cause CO poisoning. If your company does not clean chimneys, then know the names of respected chimney sweepers to recommend to your customers.

SOURCES: LENNOX, BOSTON GAS COMPANY, AND THE AMERICAN INDUSTRIAL HYGIENE ASSOCIATION

argon, helium, and carbon dioxide) has claimed many lives. The human body cannot exist for long if there is so much gas in the air that there is not enough oxygen left. This is known as "oxygen deficiency." Gases with specific gravities greater than air may lie in attics, crawl spaces, or machinery rooms for hours or days. Because these gases are colorless and odorless, they pose an immediate health hazard unless appropriate oxygen measurements and ventilation are adequately carried out.

Potentially oxygen-deficient atmospheres

Such service operations as the repair and cleaning of tanks or entry into manholes, sewers, and other confined spaces should be undertaken *only* after proper procedures for entering confined spaces have been implemented (see sidebar). These may include testing the atmosphere prior to entry, the use of lifelines, the presence of a trained observer, and ample ventilation of the enclosure. Regardless of which system is used, someone should always be stationed at the entry to see that there is no mechanical failure of equipment and to maintain constant communication with the workers inside.

Before forced ventilation is initiated, several factors must be considered, including the nature of the contaminants present, the size of the space, the type of work to be performed, and the number of people involved. Ventilation must not create additional hazards by recirculating contaminants or by substituting anything other than fresh air. (*Note:* The terms "air" and "oxygen" are sometimes considered synonymous. However, this can be a dangerous assumption, since the use of oxygen in place of fresh air for ventilation purposes will expand the limits of flammability and increase the hazards of fire or explosion.)

Careful planning is called for when you are preparing to work in a confined space. In addition to the dangers associated with hazardous atmospheres, there are other areas of concern—steam leaks, high-pressure lines, and extreme air temperatures, to name a few. Communication between the worker inside and the standby person outside is mandatory. Be sure to have adequate lighting, and make certain that there are safe entry and exit routes. Consider the use of a harness and safety line if there is any possibility that a worker will have to be removed quickly. *Always* use the utmost caution when working in a confined space.

ELECTRICAL SAFETY

Electrical safety is covered in depth in Chapter 6, but the subject is such an important one that no discussion of safety in the workplace can be complete without at least a mention of basic precautions against electrical hazards.

▶ **SAFETY TIP** ◀

Oxygen-deficient atmosphere can kill

Exposure to atmospheres containing 8 to 10% or less oxygen will bring about unconsciousness without warning, and so quickly that individuals can't help or protect themselves. Lack of sufficient oxygen may cause serious injury or death.

Never enter a suspected oxygen-deficient atmosphere without proper protective breathing apparatus and attendant support. Analyze the atmosphere to determine if there is a deficiency of oxygen. Continue to monitor during the work process. If the oxygen level is less than 19.5%, ventilate to establish good air quality.

Workers should be trained on what to expect and how to handle it. Positively isolate any incoming lines to a confined area and ventilate the area. When it's necessary to work in an oxygen-deficient atmosphere, a self-contained breathing apparatus or airline-type breathing mask should be provided for all workers.

SOURCE: COMPRESSED GAS ASSOCIATION SAFETY BULLETIN

Study the following guidelines carefully, and remember to follow them when you are working around electrical equipment:

▶ Always turn off the power before doing any work, even if only making the smallest changes that require touching exposed terminals or wires.

▶ Always lock out any disconnect that you cannot control.

▶ Never deliberately touch bare electrical wires or connections that are known to be "hot" (that is, carrying electric current) or that *could* be hot.

▶ Do not work on "hot" parts or lines unless you understand them. If it is absolutely necessary to work on a piece of equipment with "hot" lines, exercise every possible precaution.

▶ Take off all rings, watches, and jewelry.

▶ Do not stand on wet ground or floors.

▶ Do not lean against wet or damp walls or grounded machines.

▶ Always keep your hands and gloves dry.

▶ Do not put both hands on "live" parts at the same time.

▶ Never use extension cords that are worn or frayed. Make sure that the extension cord is of the proper capacity (to prevent fires and possible shock and burn hazards).

▶ Always use grounded or double-insulated power tools. (Most power tools today are of the double-insulated type—that is, they do not require a separate ground. A grounded tool has a third prong on the plug.)

▶ Never bypass fuses. Always replace a bad fuse with one of the proper size, type, and rating.

▶ Always be cautious and watchful. Pay very close attention to what you are doing.

Lockout/tagout procedures

It is obvious that a technician should never work on a piece of machinery while the power is still on, but opening the main switch is not always enough to ensure safety. Someone else may be unaware of the situation and close the

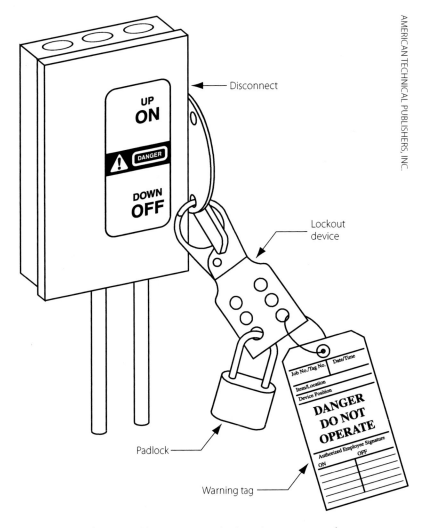

▲ **Figure 2** *Observe proper lockout/tagout procedures*

AMERICAN TECHNICAL PUBLISHERS, INC.

switch while you are still working on the equipment. OSHA has established a lockout/tagout standard (29 CFR 1910.147), which states that a piece of equipment must be turned off and disconnected from its power source prior to servicing. There are four steps:

1. Notify everyone concerned that you will be working on the equipment.
2. Turn off the power, and attach the lockout device (see Figure 2 on the previous page) to the circuit breaker or disconnect switch.
3. Put your own padlock on the lockout device and lock it with your own key. If there are other technicians working on the same job, they should add their own personally assigned locks.
4. Tag the equipment with appropriate warning signs, stating that the equipment is not to be energized or operated and that locks, tags, and other safeguards are not to be tampered with or removed until work is completed (see Figure 3).

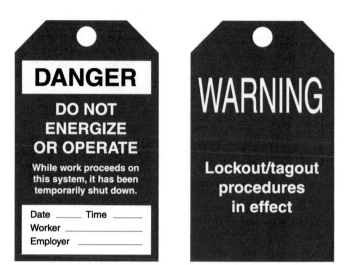

▲ *Figure 3* Sample warning tags

The electrical system must be de-energized and may need to be grounded temporarily. All hydraulic and pneumatic systems must be depressurized, tested, and locked out before work begins. (For proper lockout/tagout, all energy sources must be taken into consideration.) When you are done with your work, you may remove your lock. *Never* remove another worker's lock or tag, and never allow anyone else to remove yours for you.

If lockout is not possible, the equipment being worked on must be disabled. Often this can be done by removing fuses in the control panel. You can disable the control circuit to the magnetic starter, but this is not as safe as pulling fuses. Depending on the equipment involved, there may be other ways to disable the unit (in addition to opening the main disconnect switch).

SAFETY FIRST

Safety on the job is no accident. Common sense, good judgment, and constant alertness are necessary. Keep your mind on your job. Never cut corners in an attempt to save time, and *never* take unnecessary risks. Remember that when *you* work safe, you help keep others safe, too. If you work alone, keep a cell phone with you so that you can call for help in an emergency.

In summary, the best way to ensure workplace safety may be to recall the handy acronym A.B.C.—*always be careful!* ■

Personal Protective Equipment

INTRODUCTION

The Occupational Safety and Health Administration (OSHA) requires the use of *personal protective equipment* (PPE) to reduce employee exposure to workplace hazards. Although OSHA puts the burden of developing a comprehensive safety and health program on the employer, technicians working in the field must take some responsibility for their own safety and for the safety of those around them. The technician is sometimes the only person on a job site, and therefore the only person who can make a true determination of what hazards exist on that job. Always remember that the most important piece of personal protective equipment is *knowledge*. As a technician, you must become aware of what kinds of potential hazards exist and the best methods of protecting against those hazards.

HAZARD ASSESSMENT

A first critical step in determining which types of PPE are necessary in a given situation is to identify the hazards present on the job site. This process is known as a "hazard assessment." Potential hazards may be physical or health-related, and a comprehensive hazard assessment should identify hazards in both categories. Examples of *physical* hazards include moving objects, fluctuating temperatures, high-intensity lighting, rolling or pinching objects, electrical connections, and sharp edges. Examples of *health* hazards include overexposure to harmful dusts, chemicals, or radiation. Begin your hazard assessment with a walk-through survey of the worksite to develop a list of potential hazards in the following basic hazard categories:

▶ impact
▶ penetration

▼ **Table 1** *Hazard assessment*

Type of hazard	Examples of hazard	Common related tasks
Impact	Flying objects such as large chips, fragments, particles, sand, and dirt	Chipping, grinding, machining, masonry work, woodworking, sawing, drilling, chiseling, powered fastening, riveting, and sanding
Heat	Anything emitting extreme heat	Furnace operations, pouring, casting, hot dipping, and welding
Chemicals	Splash, fumes, vapors, and irritating mists	Acid and chemical handling, degreasing, plating, and working with blood
Dust	Harmful dust	Woodworking, buffing, and general dusty conditions
Optical radiation	Radiant energy, glare, and intense light	Welding, torch-cutting, brazing, soldering, and laser work

▶ compression (roll-over)
▶ chemical
▶ heat/cold
▶ harmful dust
▶ light (optical) radiation
▶ biological.

In addition to noting the basic layout of the job site and reviewing any history of occupational illnesses or injuries, things to look for during the walk-through survey include:
▶ sources of electricity
▶ sources of motion, such as machines or processes where movement may exist that could result in an impact between personnel and equipment
▶ sources of high temperatures that could result in burns, eye injuries, or fire
▶ types of chemicals used in the workplace
▶ sources of harmful dusts
▶ sources of light radiation, such as welding, brazing, cutting, furnaces, heat treating, high-intensity lights, etc.
▶ the potential for falling or dropping objects
▶ sharp objects that could poke, cut, stab, or puncture
▶ biological hazards, such as blood or other potentially infected material.

Table 1 summarizes some of the various types of hazards to look for during a hazard assessment.

EYE AND FACE PROTECTION

Eye protection is one of the most important precautions to be taken in any kind of service or installation work. Eye and face protection should be used any time there is potential exposure to hazards from flying particles, molten metal, liquid chemicals, acid or caustic liquids, chemical gases or vapors, or potentially injurious light radiation. For the HVACR technician, one or more of these hazards will be present most of the time from various operations that may be taking place. It is therefore essential for proper protection to be provided.

NORTH SAFETY PRODUCTS

▲ **Figure 1** *Safety glasses with side shields*

There is always some hazard of refrigerant or oil spray from the system, hoses, or cylinders during general service work, as well as the potential for small particles to fly from cutting, drilling, screwing, or other basic operations. For this type of work, a minimum of safety glasses with side shields should be worn (see Figure 1). If you wear prescription lenses, you may want to get prescription safety lenses with snap-on side shields for comfort, or a pair of safety glasses that can be worn over the prescription glasses.

The majority of impact injuries result from flying or falling objects, or from sparks striking the eye. Most of these objects are smaller than a pin head but can cause serious injury such as punctures, abrasions, and contusions. In hazardous areas where the worker is exposed to flying objects, fragments, and particles, *primary* protective devices such as safety glasses with side shields or goggles must be worn. Face shields or similar *secondary* protective devices are required in conjunction with primary protective devices during severe exposure to impact hazards.

For work overhead, work in dusty environments, or work that involves the use of powder-actuated tools, goggles that provide full enclosure should be worn (see Figure 2). Goggles with indirect vent ports help prevent dust and particles from entering while allowing some air movement to reduce fogging.

NORTH SAFETY PRODUCTS

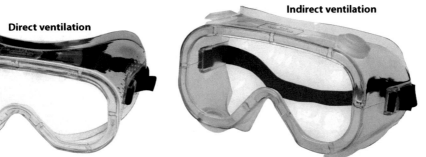

Direct ventilation

Indirect ventilation

◀ **Figure 2** *Safety goggles*

Because they create a protective seal around the eyes, safety goggles are the only effective type of eye protection from nuisance dust.

When you are working with chemicals, such as acids or alkaline cleaners used to clean condenser coils, there is always a risk of splashing chemicals on your face or into your eyes. For this type of work, full face shields should be worn (see Figure 3).

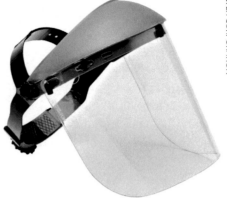

ELVEX CORPORATION

▲ **Figure 3** Face shield

A large percentage of eye injuries are caused by direct contact with chemicals. These injuries often result from an inappropriate choice of PPE that allows a chemical substance to enter from around or under protective eye equipment. Serious and irreversible damage can occur when chemical substances contact the eyes in the form of splash, mists, vapors, or fumes. When working with or around chemicals, it's important to know the location of emergency eyewash stations and how to access them with restricted vision. If an eyewash station is not available, cold tap water may be used until assistance can be obtained. It's also a good idea to carry a first aid kit in your toolbox or in your vehicle, and to make sure that it contains eyewash solution.

Table 2 lists the proper PPE devices for various types of eye and face hazards. When fitted and worn correctly, goggles can and do protect your eyes from hazardous substances. A face shield may be required in areas where you are exposed to severe chemical hazards. Operations involving soldering, brazing, arc welding, torch welding, or cutting operations require the additional use of properly shaded eye protection to prevent injury from light radiation (see Table 3). Welding helmets (see Figure 4 on page 26) also provide face protection from potential weld spatter. Safety glasses should be worn under the helmet to protect the eyes when the helmet is lifted to inspect the weld or remove slag.

Comfort is also an important factor that should be considered when you are selecting eye protection. If your safety glasses do not fit well, fog up

▼ **Table 2** Eye and face PPE devices

Impact hazards	
Safety glasses	Primary protectors intended to shield the eyes from a variety of impact hazards
Goggles	Primary protectors intended to shield the eyes against flying fragments, objects, large chips, and particles
Face shields	Secondary protectors intended to protect the entire face against exposure to impact hazards
Dust hazards	
Goggles	Primary protectors intended to protect the eyes against a variety of airborne particles and harmful dust
Chemical hazards	
Goggles	Primary protectors intended to shield the eyes against liquid or chemical splash, irritating mists, vapors, and fumes
Face shields	Secondary protectors intended to protect the entire face against exposure to chemical hazards

▼ **Table 3** *Filter lenses for protection against radiant energy*

Operation	Electrode size, in.	Arc current, A	Minimum* protective shade
Shielded metal arc welding	Less than ³/₃₂ ³/₃₂ to ⁵/₃₂ ⁵/₃₂ to ⁸/₃₂ More than ⁸/₃₂	Less than 60 60 to 160 160 to 250 250 to 550	7 8 10 11
Gas metal arc welding and flux cored arc welding		Less than 60 60 to 160 160 to 250 250 to 550	7 10 10 10
Gas tungsten arc welding		Less than 50 50 to 150 150 to 500	8 8 10
Air carbon	(Light)	Less than 500	10
Arc cutting	(Heavy)	500 to 1000	11
Plasma arc welding		Less than 20 20 to 100 100 to 400 400 to 800	6 8 10 11
Plasma arc cutting	(Light)** (Medium)** (Heavy)**	Less than 300 300 to 400 400 to 800	8 9 10
Torch brazing			3
Torch soldering			2
Carbon arc welding			14

Operation		Plate thickness, in.	Plate thickness, mm	Minimum* protective shade
Gas welding:	Light Medium Heavy	Less than ⅛ ⅛ to ½ More than ½	Less than 3.2 3.2 to 12.7 More than 12.7	4 5 6
Oxygen cutting:	Light Medium Heavy	Less than 1 1 to 6 More than 6	Less than 25 25 to 150 More than 150	3 4 5

* As a rule of thumb, start with a shade that is too dark to see the weld zone. Then go to a lighter shade that gives sufficient view of the weld zone without going below the minimum. For oxyfuel gas welding or cutting in which the torch produces a high yellow light, it is desirable to use a filter lens that absorbs the yellow or sodium line in the visible light of the (spectrum) operation.
** These values apply where the actual arc is clearly seen. Experience has shown that lighter filters may be used when the arc is hidden by the workpiece.

continuously, and are not comfortable, odds are you aren't going to like wearing them—and they don't do much good if they're left in the truck or shop.

RESPIRATORY PROTECTION

The first step toward proper respiratory protection is to be aware of those activities that are capable of generating respiratory hazards. In many cases a respiratory hazard can be eliminated by proper ventilation, the use of less toxic or less hazardous products, and proper service practices. Whenever possible, the respiratory hazard should be eliminated. When a respiratory hazard cannot be eliminated, respirators must be used.

Respirators fall into one of two general categories, generally referred to as *air-purifying* respirators and *supplied-air* respirators. The *air-purifying* type removes contaminants such as dusts and certain chemicals from the existing air. If the environment does not contain sufficient levels of oxygen or if the concentration of contaminants is too high, then a supplied-air respirator must be used.

Dusts are often produced in working with insulations, cutting processes, grinding, and sanding. Proper ventilation or other methods, such as wetting, should be used to keep the dust to a minimum. The technician must be aware that many buildings built prior to 1980 may have some insulation or transite duct work that may contain asbestos. Working with or removing asbestos materials requires special procedures for containing dust. In most states, the worker must be licensed to work with asbestos.

Dusts normally can be handled with the use of air-purifying respirators. The air-purifying respirator can range from the basic dust mask to the half-face or full-face mask with cartridge-type filters. The main difference among the respirators is how well they seal to ensure that the air breathed by the user is not bypassing the respirator.

Half-face and full-face masks provide a much better seal and a greater level of protection than a simple dust mask. Facial hair can prevent a proper seal and reduce the effectiveness of the respirator. The cartridges used in the respirators can be changed to provide protection from different types of chemicals. The cartridges typically are color-coded to identify their filtering capacity (see Table 4).

▲ *Figure 4* Welding helmet

3M/OCCUPATIONAL HEALTH & SAFETY DIVISION

▼ *Table 4* Color coding for respirator cartridges and filters

Dusts, mists, fumes	Gray
Dusts, mists, fumes, and radionuclides	Purple
Organic vapors	Black
Acid gases	White
Ammonia	Green
Acid gases and organic vapors	Yellow

WARNING: Air-purifying respirators simply remove certain airborne hazards. They do *not* increase or replenish the oxygen content of the air, and should never be worn in atmospheres containing less than 19.5% oxygen.

Supplied-air respirators must be used when there is insufficient oxygen in the atmosphere, when contaminants cannot be filtered out of the air, or when the contaminants are so concentrated that they would overload the filters. The air may be supplied by an air tank, as with the self-contained breathing apparatus (SCBA), or it may be supplied by a special compressor through a hose from outside the contaminated area.

Adequate respirators should be used whenever the air is contaminated with excessive concentrations of harmful dusts, fumes, mists, gases, or vapors. Figure 5 shows both a half-face respirator and a full-face respirator. Half-face masks are widely used with air-purifying respirators and with some supplied-air systems. Full-face masks can be used with air-purifying, powered air-purifying, and supplied-air respirators. Respirators must be cleaned any time they have lost their effectiveness. They should be taken apart, washed, dried, and defective parts replaced. Figure 6 on the next page shows a full SCBA system.

Work in environments where a respirator is needed also requires a written respiratory protection program that includes medical evaluations and proper fit testing. Most of the work of the HVACR technician does not fall into this

TYCO/SCOTT HEALTH & SAFETY

Full-face mask

Half-face mask

Replaceable filter

Exhalation valve

◀ *Figure 5*
Respirators

category. OSHA guidelines should be used to determine proper requirements.

HEAD PROTECTION

Head injuries can cause permanent impairment or even death. Hard hats can protect the head against impact, penetration, electrical shock, and burns. Wear a hard hat whenever there is a possibility that objects may fall from above, when working near low-hanging stationary objects such as pipes and valves, or when you could come into contact with electrical parts. Hard hats *always* must be worn on construction sites.

The shell of a hard hat provides not only resistance to impact and penetration, but also insulation from electric shock and electrical burns. The suspension system provides the proper fit and some shock absorption for impact. Be sure that the hard hat meets the proper class for the potential hazards.

Hard hats are divided into three industrial classes:
▶ **Class A.** Class A hard hats provide impact and penetration resistance, along with limited voltage protection (up to 2,200 V).
▶ **Class B.** Class B hard hats provide the highest level of protection against electrical hazards, with high-voltage shock and burn protection (up to 20,000 V). They also provide protection from impact and penetration hazards by flying/falling objects.
▶ **Class C.** Class C hard hats provide lightweight comfort and impact protection but offer no protection from electrical hazards.

▲ *Figure 6* Self-contained breathing apparatus (SCBA)

Another class of protective headgear on the market is called a "bump cap," designed for use in areas with low head clearance. Bump caps are recommended for areas where protection is needed from head bumps and lacerations. They are not designed to protect against falling or flying objects and are not ANSI-approved. Figure 7 shows both a hard hat and a bump cap.

Hard hats should be cleaned and inspected daily for defects. Examine both the shell and the suspension system to heat, chemicals, or ultraviolet light (such as chalking, flaking, or a loss of surface gloss). If the hard hat shows any signs of damage or excessive wear, it should be replaced immediately.

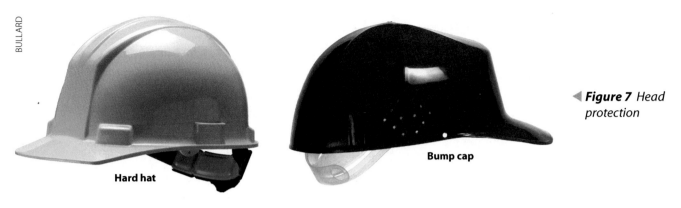

BULLARD

Hard hat

Bump cap

Figure 7 Head protection

Always replace a hard hat if it sustains an impact—the suspension system may be damaged or weakened even if the damage is not visible.

HEARING PROTECTION

Working around loud equipment or in loud environments, especially for extended periods of time, can cause permanent hearing loss. The exposure level is based on the decibel level of the sound and the length of time you are exposed to that level. When noise levels reach 90 decibels (dB), hearing protection should be worn. OSHA has established maximum exposure guidelines.

It is important to understand that the decibel scale is *logarithmic*. This means that a number 2 points higher is twice as loud, and a number 10 points higher is 10 times as loud. For example, 92 dB is twice as loud as 90 dB, and 100 dB is 10 times as loud as 90dB. Table 5 shows permissible noise exposures. Note the slight differences between U.S. and Canadian standards. Table 6 on the next page provides additional information about noise levels.

Hearing protection is generally available in three different types:
▶ *Single-use earplugs* are made of waxed cotton, foam, silicone rubber, or fiberglass wool. They are self-forming and, when properly inserted, they work as well as most molded earplugs.
▶ *Pre-formed or molded earplugs* must be individually fitted by a professional and can be disposable or reusable. Reusable plugs should be cleaned after each use.
▶ *Earmuffs* require a perfect seal around the ear. When properly fitted and worn, they provide more protection than earplugs. Eye glasses, facial hair, long hair, or facial movements such as chewing may reduce the protective value of earmuffs.

▼ *Table 5* Permissible noise exposures

Duration per day	Sound level
8 hr	90 dB
6 hr	92 dB
4 hr	95 dB
3 hr	97 dB
2 hr	100 dB
1½ hr	102 dB
1 hr	105 dB
30 min	110 dB
15 min or less	115 dB

SOURCE: OSHA

Duration per day	Sound level
8 hr	90 dB
4 hr	93 dB
2 hr	96 dB
1 hr	99 dB
30 min	102 dB
15 min	105 dB
No exposure without hearing protection	>108 dB

SOURCE: CONSTRUCTION SAFETY ASSOCIATION OF ONTARIO

Figure 8 shows various types of earplugs and earmuffs. Figure 9 shows a cap-mounted earmuff model.

Noise reduction ratings (NRR) are listed on the packaging for hearing protection devices. The higher the NRR number, the greater the protection. The exposure level minus the NRR should bring the noise level below 85 dB. It is recommended that a 50% safety factor be used with the NRR due to variations caused by fit. For example, if you know that you will be exposed to noise levels in the 100-dB range, then hearing protection with a NRR of 15 dB is necessary to reduce the risk to the acceptable 85-dB range (100 − 85 = 15). However, adding the 50% safety factor (50% of 15 = 7.5) means that you should select a hearing protection device with a NRR of 22.5 dB (15 + 7.5 = 22.5).

HAND PROTECTION

The HVACR technician faces potential hazards to the hands from cuts, abrasions, chemicals, and extreme temperatures. It is important to select hand protection that is best suited for the hazard. This means that for the best hand protection, several different types of gloves may be needed as precautions against different hazards.

Leather gloves typically provide good protection from the cuts and abrasions that can be caused by the sharp edges of equipment or sheet metal. Leather gloves also provide protection against burns that may occur from contact with hot surfaces, such as may occur during welding, cutting, soldering, brazing, or even checking the operation of a compressor or its discharge line.

Chemical exposure generally requires the use of some type of neoprene or rubber gloves to prevent contact with and absorption into the skin. The service technician often uses

▼ **Table 6** *Average sound levels*

Type of noise	Sound level
Pin drop	15 dB
Whisper	40 dB
Average office noise	50 dB
Normal conversation	60 dB
Heavy truck traffic	85 dB
Point at which hearing damage can begin	85 dB
Power tools, thunder	110 dB
Front row at a rock concert	120–130 dB
Jackhammer	125 dB
Jet engine (close up)	155 dB

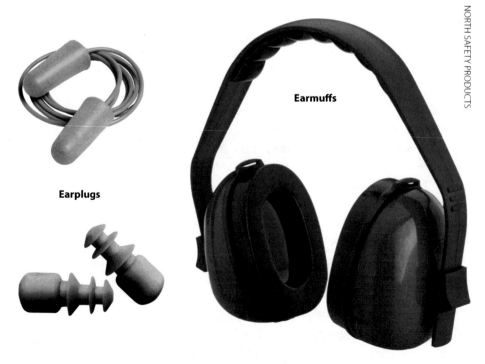

Earmuffs

Earplugs

NORTH SAFETY PRODUCTS

▲ **Figure 8** *Hearing protection*

strong acid or alkaline cleaners to clean scale and grease deposits on coils. Solvents and lubricants are used in and around heating and cooling systems. Refrigerants and other specialized chemicals also are used. The type of gloves that are being considered should be checked to ensure that they are resistant to the chemicals to which they are being exposed.

Refrigerants can pose two different hazards at the same time. Liquid refrigerant can cause immediate frostbite due to its low boiling point at atmospheric conditions. The refrigerant also may carry oils from the system that pose a spray risk during the installation or removal of hoses. The oil may be acidic in the case of a compressor burnout. For handling refrigerants, the best choice is gloves that offer both thermal protection (from the cold temperatures) and chemical protection (to prevent the oil from soaking through).

Gloves also should be worn to protect against electric shock. The type of glove required depends on the voltage of the electrical source.

ELVEX CORPORATION

▲ *Figure 9* Cap-mounted earmuffs

FOOT PROTECTION

General footwear for the HVACR technician should consist of heavy leather close-toed work shoes or boots. This type of shoe will protect the service worker from general hazards. When you are working on a construction site or installing large equipment, the risk of dropping heavy objects and crushing the toes is much greater. In such cases, steel-toed shoes should be worn. All footwear should be nonconductive to help protect against electric shock.

PROTECTIVE CLOTHING

The HVACR technician can experience extreme variations in temperature— you may be working on a rooftop unit in below-freezing weather and a few minutes later walk into a 90°F (32°C) boiler room. You not only need to dress appropriately for changes in temperature, you also need to dress to protect yourself against potential hazards.

One of the hazards that the HVACR technician faces is the potential for chemical contact while handling acid or alkaline coil or heat exchanger cleaning products or any of the variety of water treatment chemicals that may be used in boilers, cooling towers, and hydronic systems. To protect against chemical contact, the technician should wear a rubber apron or a rain suit with pants that can be washed down easily in the case of a spill.

During welding or cutting operations, sparks or a splatter of molten metal can result in burns to the skin or cause clothing to catch fire. In such cases, a heavy leather welding jacket and leggings should be added to your other PPE gear in order to provide an insulating layer.

FALL PROTECTION

How important is fall protection? An OSHA safety poster states that there are 206 reasons for fall protection—the number of bones in the human body!

Fall protection generally is required when a technician is working on a platform or any other surface (including a roof) that has more than a 6-ft (1.8-m) drop, or any time work is taking place over moving machinery, no matter what the height. Fall protection may be provided in the form of guardrails or walls at least 42 in. (1.1 m) in height.

Where a fixed form of fall protection is not provided, personal fall protection must be used. Personal fall protection also is required when technicians work on lifts that have articulating platforms.

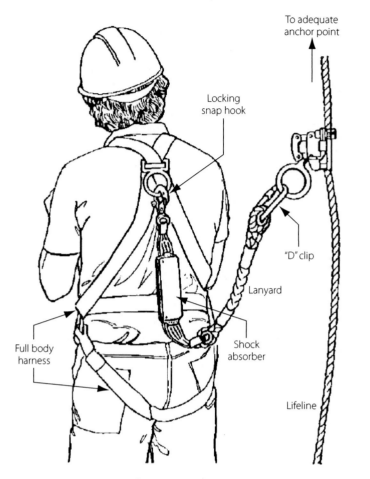

▲ *Figure 10* Fall protection

Personal fall protection generally consists of a properly fitted body harness attached to a properly anchored fall-arresting system. Body harnesses are available in different styles to accommodate different types of work (see Figure 10). In no case is a safety belt allowed to be used for fall protection. Safety belts are intended for positioning purposes only. Most body harnesses incorporate additional "D" rings so that they can serve both for positioning and fall protection.

The fall-arresting lanyard may be a shock-absorbing type, a non-shock-absorbing type, or a retractable type that locks in the case of a fall. It is extremely important to choose a solid anchoring point and one that is high enough so that by the time the decelerating lanyard opens up, you have not fallen far enough to have hit anything below you.

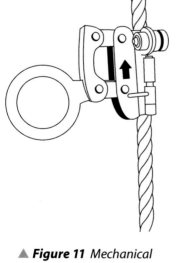

▲ *Figure 11* Mechanical rope grab

CONSTRUCTION SAFETY ASSOCIATION OF ONTARIO

CONSTRUCTION SAFETY ASSOCIATION OF ONTARIO

When you wear a full body harness, adjust the chest strap so that it is snug and located near the middle of the chest. Leg straps should be adjusted so that the user's fist can fit snugly between strap and leg. The harness straps should be adjusted so that the "D" ring or other connective device is between the shoulder blades. Before using, always inspect harnesses and lanyards for:

▶ burns, cuts, or signs of chemical damage
▶ loose or broken stitching
▶ frayed web material.

To attach a lanyard to a lifeline, use a mechanical rope grab, as shown in Figure 11. If a mechanical rope grab is not available, then use a triple sliding hitch (see Figure 12). Tie the hitch as illustrated. Be sure to allow a 12-in. (30-cm) dead end. Tighten the hitch on the lifeline so that the hitch won't slip. Position the hitch on the lifeline above head height.

The lifeline must reach the ground or a secure and accessible level above ground. It should be knotted, cable-clipped, or otherwise provided with a positive stop to keep the hitch from running off the end of the lifeline. If you fall, do not grab the hitch, lanyard, or lifeline. To work properly, the hitch must come under a load.

To ensure that your fall protection device is fully funtional and that you are using it properly, obtain the necessary training prior to your first use! ■

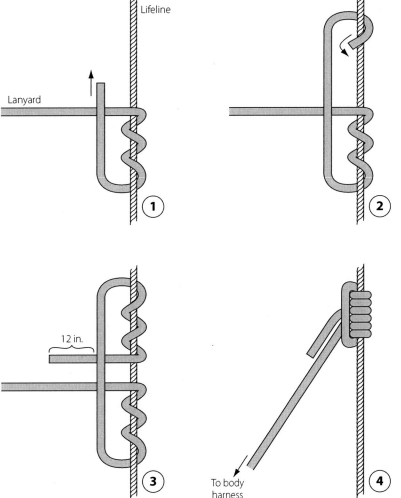

▲ **Figure 12** *Triple sliding hitch*

CONSTRUCTION SAFETY ASSOCIATION OF ONTARIO

Tools and Test Instruments

USING TOOLS PROPERLY

Many injuries occur each year due to the improper use of tools. Most of these injuries can be avoided by taking proper safety precautions. This Chapter is intended to give some guidelines for tool safety.

Most tool hazards can be eliminated by following a few basic rules:

▶ Keep your tools in good condition.

▶ Use the right tools for the job.

▶ Check tools for damage and worn parts before using them.

▶ Be familiar with your tools and use them only according to the manufacturers' instructions.

▶ Always use the proper personal protective equipment.

HAND TOOLS

Hand tools, which include a wide variety of common implements (see Figure 1), are defined as tools that are powered manually. Some of the greatest hazards associated with hand tools occur when they are used for

Figure 1 ▶
Common hand tools

STANLEY TOOLS

purposes for which they are not intended. You shouldn't use a screwdriver as a chisel or pry bar, for example. Don't use a wrench or a pair of pliers as a hammer. Since the tools are not designed for these functions, they can easily break and cause parts to fly.

Another major hazard comes from using worn or poorly maintained tools. Always check tools carefully for damage before using them. Damaged tools should be repaired or replaced immediately. Examples of hazards due to wear include:

▶ Dull cutting edges and worn screwdriver tips require more force, which in turn increases the risk of the tool slipping off the workpiece.

▶ Worn or sprung jaws on pliers or pipe wrenches also increase the likelihood of slippage.

▶ A splintered, cracked, or loose handle on a hammer or mallet may allow the head to break loose and become a projectile.

▶ The mushroomed head of a chisel may break apart, causing the pieces to fly off and strike you or someone nearby.

Always use tools properly and as intended. Here are some basic hand tool reminders:

▶ Do not use a screwdriver for prying or chiseling. Never use a screwdriver on a workpiece held in your hand—a slip could cause serious injury.

▶ Screwdriver blades must be properly sized to fit the screw slot. Screwdriver handles should be of a non-conducting material.

▶ Do not use files without handles.

▶ Do not put sharp-edged tools, such as chisels, punches, and open knives, in your pockets—even temporarily. Keep guards on the sharp edges and points of tools in tool kits.

▶ Make sure that tools are secured when working on ladders or scaffolding. Falling tools can seriously injure someone below.

▶ Never use a "cheater bar" (a piece of pipe used to extend the length of a tool handle).

▶ Use a properly sized wrench—*not* a pair of pliers—to tighten and loosen nuts and bolts.

▶ Always use sharp tools by *pushing* them *away* from you, never by *pulling* them *toward* you.

Don't forget personal protective equipment (PPE). Hand tools often "seem safer" than power tools, so it becomes easy to let down your guard. At a minimum, working with hand tools requires the use of safety glasses. Depending on the tool and the task, additional items (such as gloves) may be necessary.

OSHA hand tools and equipment checklist

Use the following checklist to make sure that your tools and your company's tool maintenance policies are safe:

☐ Are all tools and equipment (both company-owned and employee-owned) in good condition?

☐ Are hand tools such as chisels and punches, which can develop mushroomed heads during use, reconditioned or replaced as necessary?

☐ Are broken or fractured handles on hammers, axes, and similar tools replaced promptly?

☐ Are worn or bent wrenches replaced regularly?

☐ Are appropriate handles used on files and similar tools?

☐ Are employees made aware of the hazards caused by faulty or improperly used hand tools?

☐ Do service technicians wear appropriate safety glasses, face shields, etc. while using hand tools or equipment that might produce flying materials or be subject to breakage?

☐ Are tool handles wedged tightly in the heads of all tools?

☐ Are the cutting edges of tools kept sharp so that the tools will move smoothly, without binding or skipping?

☐ Are tools stored in a secure location where they won't be tampered with?

NON-SPARKING TOOLS

If you are working around flammable material, sparks from steel tools may provide an ignition source. When working in this type of hazardous environment, non-sparking tools made from brass, plastic, aluminum, wood, or other materials should be used.

POWER TOOLS

Power tools are usually electric or battery-powered, but can also be powered by compressed air, a gasoline engine, hydraulic force, or some other means. The risks associated with using these tools is greatly elevated due to the significant power that they produce and the high speeds at which they can operate. Technicians often become far too comfortable working with these tools and forget to follow basic safety precautions.

When using portable electric tools, use a three-wire cord. One wire is the *hot* (black), one is the *neutral* (white), and the remaining conductor is the *ground* (green), which is connected to the tool frame. It is always a good practice—and a requirement on construction sites—to use *ground fault circuit interrupters* (GFCIs) for your power tools. This type of receptacle, shown in Figure 2 on the next page, provides a greater level of protection for the user of power hand tools against electric shock.

▶ **SAFETY TIP** ◀

Caution counts when using power tools

Following are some tips for the safe operation of power-operated hand tools:

▷ Be sure that safety guards are in working order and in place before operating any power tool.

▷ Clamp or otherwise secure small or light materials to free both hands before attempting to ream, drill, tap, or perform similar operations.

▷ Keep moving parts of power tools pointed away from your body. Do not hold a finger on the power switch while carrying a plugged-in tool.

▷ Take special precautions when using power tools on a scaffold or other locations with limited space. Get good footing, use both hands, keep cords clear of obstructions, and do not overreach.

▷ Be sure that a power tool is off and motion is stopped before setting it down.

▷ When drilling into walls, floors, platforms, and similar structures, know what you are drilling into. Take care not to drill into electrical and other utility lines and other such installations.

▷ Disconnect tools from power source(s) before changing blades or bits, or attempting repair or adjustment. Never leave a running tool unattended.

SOURCE: MCAA SAFETY MANUAL FOR THE MECHANICAL TRADES

Shock protection is very important, since work is often done in damp locations or around metal parts and equipment (such as ductwork, air handlers, and cooling towers) that conduct electricity very well and can provide a ground path. Even if a shock is not severe enough to be the direct cause of damage or injury itself, it can trigger a reaction that may cause the person to fall from a ladder or other elevated surface. Observe the following precautions when working with electric tools:

▶ Never carry a tool by its cord. Never use cords for hoisting or lowering tools.

▶ Never yank the cord to unplug it from the receptacle.

▶ Never operate a tool with the ground plug missing.

▶ Protect cords from heat, oils, and sharp edges.

▶ Run extension cords in a manner that will reduce the risk of tripping over them.

▶ Before plugging any tool into an electrical outlet, make sure that the tool switch is off. Surprise and accidental start-ups are dangerous.

▶ Always turn tools off before unplugging them.

BRYANT ELECTRIC

Test button

Steady ON green LED indicates power (no power present when reverse-wired)

Reset button

Flashing red LED signals loss of GFCI protection

Steady ON red LED signals ground fault condition

▲ *Figure 2* GFCI receptacle with LED indicators

Power hand tools should be inspected on a regular basis to ensure that they are in good shape and electrically sound. Any faulty power hand tools should be repaired or replaced immediately. GFCIs should be tested each time they are used.

A power tool should always be used within the limits for which it was intended, to prevent both added risk to the user and damage to the tool. Tools should be cleaned, lubricated, and maintained according to the manufacturer's instructions to ensure that they will operate properly and safely. Damaged tools should be removed from service immediately and repaired or replaced. *Always unplug tools before cleaning, making repairs, or changing accessories.*

When you use any power tool, wear PPE that is appropriate for the tool and the task. You must evaluate each tool and job separately to determine proper PPE. Eye protection is a necessity. In some cases, full face protection may be more appropriate. Gloves may increase the potential hazard of getting a hand or arm caught in the rotating parts of a tool, and need to be considered carefully. Do not wear rings, jewelry, or loose-fitting clothing that could get caught in the moving parts of a machine.

Extension cords

Cords on power tools should be inspected on a regular basis to ensure that there are no cuts, missing insulation, or damaged plugs that could cause electric shock to the user. Extension cords used with power tools also must be checked for damage on a regular basis and must be sized properly for the tool. A cord that is too small or too long will result in excessive voltage drop, causing both the cord and the tool to overheat. Observe the following safety precautions when using extension cords:

▶ All extension cords must be of the outdoor type, rated for 600 V, and have an insulated grounding conductor.

▶ Defective cords and cords with frayed insulation must not be used. Replace damaged cords immediately.

▶ Extension cords that are in use must be protected from damage caused by sharp edges, traffic, flame cutting, materials handling, and other operations.

▶ In areas where there are potential dangers (such as metal enclosures or damp locations), extension cords should be used only with approved ground fault protection.

Remember: Your life may depend on the condition of the hand tools and extension cords that you use every day.

OSHA portable (power-operated) tool and equipment checklist

Use the following checklist to evaluate power tool safety:

☐ Are grinders, saws, and similar equipment provided with appropriate safety guards?

☐ Are power tools used with the correct shields, guards, or attachments, as recommended by the manufacturer?

☐ Are portable circular saws equipped with guards above and below the base shoe?

☐ Are circular saw guards checked to ensure that they are not wedged up, thus leaving the lower portion of the blade unguarded?

☐ Are rotating or moving parts of equipment guarded to prevent physical contact?

☐ Are all cord-connected, electrically operated tools and equipment effectively grounded, or of the approved double-insulated type?

☐ Are effective guards in place over belts, pulleys, chains, and sprockets on such equipment as air compressors?

▶ SAFETY TIP ◀

Four steps to ensure power tool safety

Follow these four steps when working with portable power tools:

1. Wear proper PPE. Your hands and eyes are priceless. Wear protective clothing to prevent cuts and burns. Always wear safety glasses when there is danger of flying wood, metal, or other particles.

2. Inspect and test. Before you use any power tool, check it for broken or loose parts. If you're using a tool with a sharp edge, use a scrap of wood—not your fingers—to test its sharpness.

3. Start from "off." Before plugging in a power tool, check the power switch to make sure that it's in the "off" position. It's dangerous to plug in a tool when the switch is "on." When you're finished, make sure the tool has stopped before unplugging it and putting it down.

4. Prevent shock. Be sure that tools are properly grounded and double-insulated. Keep cords away from heat, sharp objects, and chemicals that could damage their insulation. Keep your work area dry. If you must work in a wet area, keep the power cord clear of wet surfaces and use a GFCI.

SOURCE: NATIONAL AIR DUCT CLEANERS ASSOCIATION SAFETY MANUAL

□ Are portable fans provided with full guards or screens that have openings of ½ in. (1.3 cm) or less?

□ Are GFCIs provided on all temporary electric 15- and 20-A circuits used during periods of construction?

□ Are pneumatic and hydraulic hoses on power-operated tools checked regularly for deterioration or damage?

Cordless tools

Battery-operated tools (see Figure 3) eliminate many of the hazards related to working with power cords and higher voltages. The amount of power that a battery-operated tool produces and the duration of its operation are limited by the size of the battery. The most significant hazard from the batteries comes from the potential for damage—or even explosion—due to overheating. This type of overheating is generally caused by shorting out the battery or by improper charging.

Batteries should be stored with protective caps in place. This practice prevents the possibility of conductive material coming in contact with the battery terminals, which can create a short.

A battery should be recharged *only* in the manufacturer's charger designed for that specific type of battery. Attempting to charge the battery in the incorrect charger can lead to it rapidly overheating. Always inspect batteries for physical damage before using them or placing them in a charging unit. A battery with a cracked or bulging case should be discarded immediately. Always dispose of batteries in a proper manner. Many places that sell batteries have recycling programs and can properly dispose of your old batteries.

BOSCH

▲ **Figure 3** *Typical cordless drill*

TOOL GUARDS

Tool guards are intended to reduce the potential for accidental contact with the moving parts of power tools, and to protect the operator from flying chips or sparks. Tool guards cover belts, gears, shafts, pulleys, saw blades, cutting wheels, and grinding wheels. Such tools should *never* be operated unless guards are in place and properly adjusted.

PNEUMATIC TOOLS

Pneumatic tools are very similar to electric power tools, but pneumatic tools use compressed air as the source of power. The majority of safety precautions that apply to other power tools also apply to pneumatic tools, with a few changes relating to the power source:

▶ Pressures should be checked and set to match the tool manufacturer's specifications.

▶ A pressure relief valve should be in place and tested daily to protect against dangerous pressures.

▶ Air hoses should be checked daily for cracks, splits, or "alligatoring" that could cause them to fail.

▶ Air hoses must be securely fastened to the tools so that they will not come loose and whip around. An air hose more than ½ in. in diameter must have a safety excess flow valve installed at the source of the air supply to reduce the pressure in case of hose failure.

▶ Tools should have retainers to prevent ejection of the tool.

▶ Air hoses must be disconnected before repairs or adjustments are made on the tool.

GASOLINE-POWERED TOOLS

The use of gasoline-powered tools brings with it the additional hazards of handling, transporting, and storing a flammable liquid. You must use *only* containers designed for storing flammable liquids. Store containers away from ignition sources and keep only the minimum amount of fuel necessary for the tool. Follow all safety precautions related to grounding when filling containers and always shut off equipment and allow it to cool before filling. A fire extinguisher should always be kept on hand.

A second hazard resulting from the use of tools powered by gasoline engines comes from the exhaust fumes. *These types of tools should be used only in well-ventilated areas to prevent carbon monoxide poisoning.*

POWDER-ACTUATED TOOLS

A powder-actuated tool works much like a gun, in that it uses an explosive shell to fire a fastener into concrete or steel. These tools can be extremely dangerous when used by people who have not been properly trained in their safe operation. High-velocity and low-velocity powder-actuated tools exist. In general, a low-velocity tool should always be used—it provides the same function but is much safer to operate.

Operation of a powder-actuated tool requires two motions to prevent accidental firing. First, the barrel must be brought to the firing position and pressed against the surface with at least 5 lb of force. Then the trigger is pulled to fire the round. In case of misfire, the tool should be held in place for at least 30 seconds and then the load should be removed and placed in water. Always take the tool out of service immediately if it is damaged or malfunctioning in any way.

Proper PPE must be worn when working with this type of tool. Eye protection must always be worn to protect against dust and flying particles. Due to the high level of sound produced by the firing of the load, hearing protection should always be worn as well. The guidelines below provide additional safety precautions for powder-actuated tools:

- ▶ Do not use a powder-actuated tool in an explosive atmosphere.
- ▶ Fully inspect the tool before using.
- ▶ Do not load the tool until you are ready to use it.
- ▶ Do not leave the loaded tool unattended.
- ▶ Keep hands, feet, and all other body parts clear of the barrel end.
- ▶ *Never* point the tool at anyone.
- ▶ Do not fire fasteners into materials that might allow the fasteners to pass through to the other side.
- ▶ Do not fire into very brittle materials that might chip, splatter, or cause the fasteners to ricochet.

OSHA powder-actuated tool checklist

Use the following checklist to aid you in using powder-actuated tools safely:

- ☐ Are employees who operate powder-actuated tools trained in their use? Does each user carry a valid operator's card?
- ☐ Is each powder-actuated tool stored in its own locked container when not being used?
- ☐ Is a sign at least 7 in. × 10 in. (17.8 cm × 25.4 cm) with bold-face type reading **POWDER-ACTUATED TOOL IN USE** conspicuously posted when the tool is being used?
- ☐ Are powder-actuated tools left unloaded until they are ready to be used?
- ☐ Are powder-actuated tools inspected for obstructions or defects each day before use?
- ☐ Do powder-actuated tool operators have and use appropriate PPE such as hard hats, safety goggles, safety shoes, and ear protectors?

TEST METERS

Test meters are used for a variety of purposes—from taking voltage readings to measuring air flow to checking for the presence of carbon monoxide and combustible gases. Electronic test instruments are probably the most delicate and sensitive tools that you carry with you. There will be times when your life and safety (and that of others around you) depend on this equipment functioning properly—and on you using it correctly. Figure 4 shows a typical multimeter.

Even the same types of meters vary from manufacturer to manufacturer, so it is extremely important that you read the instructions regarding the use and

---

▶ SAFETY TIP ◀

Practice multimeter safety to avoid possible injury

Momentary high-voltage transients or spikes can travel through a multimeter at any time and without warning. Motors, capacitors, lightning, and power conversion equipment such as variable-speed drives are all possible sources of spikes. Important tips to know in the safe use of multimeters include:

- ▷ Ensure that the meter's voltage rating is appropriate for the work being done.
- ▷ Use PPE such as eye protection, flame-resistant clothing, long-sleeve shirt, dielectric safety boots, rubber gloves with leather protectors, mats, blankets, and shields.
- ▷ Check the manufacturer's manual for specific cautions. Moisture and cold may affect the performance of your meter.
- ▷ Wipe the multimeter and test leads clean to remove any surface contamination prior to use.
- ▷ Start with high ranges of the multimeter, then move to the lower ranges when the values to be measured are uncertain.
- ▷ Connect to ground first and disconnect to ground last.
- ▷ Test the multimeter on a known power source to verify the meter's proper function before and after testing the suspect circuit.

SOURCE: CONSTRUCTION SAFETY ASSOCIATION OF ONTARIO

care of your particular meter. Improper use of the equipment can give you false or inaccurate readings, which can be just as dangerous as a meter that does not function properly. You should spend some time getting to know your meter by testing some non-critical item before you need to use it in a potentially life-threatening situation.

Proper care and calibration of your test equipment is also extremely important. Again, you must check the operating instructions, since requirements vary for different types of equipment. Some meters can be calibrated in the field, while others need to be sent back to the factory or service center. Some types of equipment have sensors that must be replaced on a regular basis.

Test equipment should be checked against a known source to ensure that the meter is working correctly. For example, an electrical meter should be checked against a live circuit to verify that it is working before it is used to verify that the power is turned off. After verifying that the power is off, the meter should be checked on a live source again. Likewise, a gas leak detector can be placed near a known source of gas to verify that it is reading. Be sure to check your instruction manual to prevent meter damage, however—exposing a carbon monoxide meter to high levels of carbon monoxide can damage or shorten the life of the sensor.

Electrical meters are sensitive to extreme temperatures and high humidity levels. Let the meter "climatize" to the surrounding conditions before using it. Cold temperatures may affect the digital display, while high humidity or wet conditions may cause internal damage to the meter.

Always use the right meter for the job. Make sure that electrical meters have a high enough voltage rating for the work to be done and a minimum CAT III safety rating. Electrical meter safety is discussed in more detail in Chapter 6. Whatever the condition you are checking, make sure that the meter is capable of reading within the range that you need to measure. ■

FLUKE CORPORATION

▲ *Figure 4* Typical *digital multimeter*

Electrical Safety

ELECTRICAL INJURIES

Electric currents, regardless of how small the current values are and whether they are encountered in the workplace or elsewhere, may be sufficient to cause serious harm, such as burns (both internal and external), blindness, and a variety of injuries related to falls. Obviously, the worse-case scenario is death by electrocution.

Workers in the HVACR industry make a living working with and around electricity. During the installation, maintenance, and repair of both high- and low-voltage systems, service technicians are constantly exposed to environments that may be potentially dangerous (see Figure 1). It is important to understand and recognize electrical hazards, as well as methods of preventing electric shocks, related injuries, and electrocution.

On average, one worker in North America is electrocuted every day, making electrocution one of the leading causes of death in the workplace, especially among young workers. Over half of all electrocutions and electrical injuries are suffered by workers who are working on systems with voltages of less than 600 V ac.

Figure 1 ▶
*Be aware of
electrical hazards*

DANGER
Electrocution risk

DANGER
ELECTROCUTION HAZARD
KEEP CLEAR
DEATH OR SERIOUS INJURY CAN RESULT FROM
CONTACT WITH THIS EQUIPMENT IF IT SHOULD
BECOME ELECTRICALLY CHARGED

DANGER
**Do not
switch on**

When direct bodily contact is made with electric current, the body creates an alternative, lower-resistance path for the current to flow through—instead of the intended path (see Figure 2). The human body can provide resistance values from as low as 100 Ω to as high as 1,000,000 Ω. This vast range of resistance depends on whether the skin is wet or dry, broken or intact. Although current flow has difficulty passing through the higher body resistance values, it will seek out and flow through the lower resistance values easily.

The amount of water content (fat versus muscle) also affects the resistance of the human body to electric current. If the resistance of the skin is high enough at the time of an accident to prevent electric current from traveling through the body, one can be considered to be very fortunate. Remember: the lower the resistance—due to wet hands or feet, cuts and scrapes, etc.—the higher the current flow into and through the body!

Burns caused by electric current flowing through the body are the result of the current "breaking through" the skin as it enters and leaves the body. These burns are usually visible, but in many cases the entry/exit points may be so small that no external marks are visible. Even though it may appear that no outward harm has been done, damage beneath the skin can become life-threatening. This damage may include clotted blood vessels, "cooking" of the blood, vaporization of muscle tissue, severe internal organ damage, and nerve and/or brain damage. These conditions frequently are not evident at first, and may not be discovered until medical expertise becomes available. But such injuries can produce lifelong disabilities or death.

Other types of injuries caused by electric shock are the results of falls from ladders, scaffolds, roofs, or other elevated platforms. Without proper harnessing and protection, even a small electric

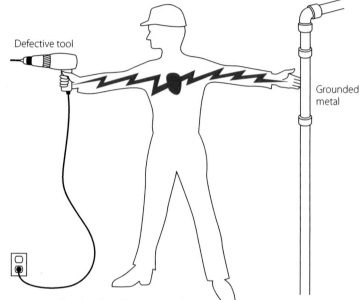

Defective tool

Grounded metal

Hand-to-hand current path

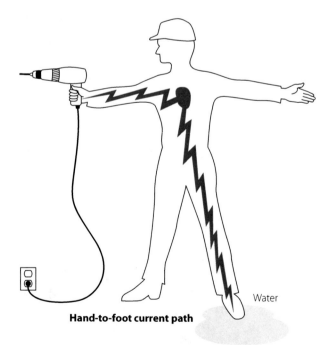

Water

Hand-to-foot current path

▲ **Figure 2** *Death can result when electric current passes through your heart* shock may cause a reaction or involuntary muscle movement that leads to a slip or a fall, possibly resulting in death.

Many people associate electrocution and other electrical injuries with high-voltage power supplies. *This is absolutely false!* Electrocution and injuries resulting from electric shock can occur at *any* voltage, provided that the appropriate current is present. It is true that in many cases, contact with higher voltages results in severe injuries and a greater number of deaths—but this is due to the higher current levels available. At first glance, lower voltages may not appear to be very dangerous, but if the conditions are right the results can be fatal. Table 1 shows the results on the human body of different current levels. *Note that there is no mention of voltage supply*, since these currents may be present at any voltage, regardless of how large or small.

Electric shocks

In order to receive an electric shock, your body must act as a conductor, providing a complete path or circuit through which the current can travel. This is normally accomplished when you touch a bare, live ("hot") wire or a live component with one part of your body while another part of your body comes into contact with an electrical ground or a wire or component with a different voltage potential. If your body becomes the path of least resistance, the current will pass through both external and internal body parts to complete a circuit, instead of taking the normal path (the intended circuit through the wiring, components, etc.).

▼ **Table 1** *Effects of electric current on human body*

Current	Effect on body
1 mA	Slight tingle Usually no visible marks on skin Normally no bodily damage
2 to 9 mA	Slight shock sensation Usually not painful May cause involuntary muscle action May result in fall from elevated surface
10 to 24 mA	Painful shock Burns may be visible at point of entry Loss of muscular control "Freezing action" (unable to let go of object conducting current)
25 to 74 mA	Extremely painful Visible entry and exit burns Severe muscle contractions Breathing may stop Death is possible
75 to 300 mA	Muscle contraction Nerve damage Ventricular fibrillation Death is likely
Over 300 mA	Severe burns Burned limbs may require amputation Cardiac arrest Death is highly likely
Over 1 A	Life-threatening burns Heart paralysis Death is highly likely
15 A	(Lowest fuse or circuit breaker size) Effects and injuries may vary according to specific conditions and length of exposure

As mentioned previously, the amount of resistance the body offers to electric current can vary tremendously. The amount of moisture or perspiration on your skin, the amount of moisture in the air, standing on a concrete floor, standing in a pool of water, the type of clothing being worn—all of these factors can change the resistance around your body.

The actual path of current through the body and the length of time the body must endure the current determine the amount and extent of injury suffered. For example, if current flows from your finger to your elbow (of the same arm), you may experience severe pain. However, the same amount of current passing through your heart and lungs can cause ventricular fibrillation, cardiac arrest, or possibly death. The difference lies in nonvital body parts versus vital body parts.

The most severe—and potentially fatal—circuit for electric current is one that passes directly through the heart, which causes the heart to beat erratically and, possibly, stop. In many cases, current traveling this path also flows through several other vital organs, causing extensive damage and lifelong injuries. If death does not occur instantaneously, it may follow as a result of complications. The flow of current from arm to arm, arm to foot, arm to head, or head to foot are typically the most damaging and fatal.

Electrical burns

Burns are the most common nonfatal injuries produced by electric shocks. In many cases, visual marks are left on the skin. Burns from severe electric shocks and arcs can be very dangerous and even fatal.

A burn resulting from the direct contact of an electric current with the skin normally requires immediate medical attention. Electric current that passes through clothing may ignite the clothing, which means that the wearer can suffer severe thermal burns from the fire. That is why it is advisable to wear clothing of a fire-resistant material when you are working around electricity. This includes both natural and synthetic clothing materials.

Other forms of burns are caused when high-amperage current travels through the air as an arc, producing temperatures as high as 35,000°F (19,427°C). At these temperatures, the intense heat and light can cause damage to skin and eyesight, as well as vaporization and ignition of non-fire-retardant clothing. Pressure waves (also known as the explosion effect) may develop as a result of such high-voltage arcs, causing ear damage and concussions. Persons thrown or knocked down by the arc blast may suffer broken bones, bruising, or death.

High-voltage arcs also may cause electrical components to explode, sending fragments and molten metal in all directions and possibly injuring workers. In addition, arcs can lead to the combustion of gases, vapors, or dust, causing explosions, fires, and other related concerns.

PRECAUTIONS AGAINST ELECTRICAL HAZARDS

Most tools and pieces of electrical equipment, especially if they have been approved by the Underwriters Laboratories (UL) or Canadian Standards Association (CSA), are provided with adequate protective insulation, barriers, and safety devices. But these cannot protect against unsafe, careless, and "take-a-chance" practices by those who install, repair, service, maintain, or operate the equipment. *Your own carefulness and watchfulness are your best protectors.*

Common sense dictates that you should never unnecessarily touch bare electrical wires or connections that are known to be "hot"—that is, carrying electric current. If possible, disconnect and lock the circuit switch, so that the line is dead before working on it. If it is necessary to work with "hot" lines or equipment, use every precaution:

▶ Do not work on "hot" parts or lines unless you understand them.
▶ Do not stand on wet floors or earth.
▶ Keep your hands and gloves dry.
▶ Do not lean against damp walls or grounded machines.
▶ Do not put both hands on live parts at the same time.
▶ Be vigilant.

IDENTIFYING ELECTRICAL HAZARDS

By remembering the two basic conditions required to receive an electric shock, you should be able to view a situation and assess whether it presents any visible or potential electrical hazards. The two things that you must keep foremost in your mind at all times are:

▶ Avoid having your body become an alternative path of least resistance.
▶ Never expose your body to two different voltage potentials (i.e., live wire to ground, live wire to live wire, etc.).

To help avoid these potentially dangerous situations, the following paragraphs offer a view of various scenarios.

Fuses and circuit breakers

What is the function of fuses and circuit breakers? First, to protect the wiring connected to the equipment. Second, to protect the equipment loads. And *last*, to protect health and life. When you recognize the fact that 25 mA

▶ SAFETY TIP ◀

Follow electrical safety rules

By following basic safety rules, technicians can avoid most electrical accidents. The first line of defense against accidents involving electricity is to keep yourself from becoming a conductor. Thus:

▷ Stay dry. Avoid working on electrical equipment when you're wet or if your shoes are wet.
▷ Don't stand in puddles or on wet ground. If possible, stand on a rubber mat or dry wooden platform when you work on electrical equipment.
▷ Wear rubber-soled shoes.
▷ Don't wear a watch, ring, or other metal jewelry. They can catch in machinery, conduct electricity, and they can cause a severe burn as electricity arcs between the body and the metal.
▷ Avoid contact with metal pipes—they provide a perfect ground.
▷ Use a ladder made of wood or fiberglass, not metal.
▷ If you must work around energized circuits, use one hand only. If both hands are in contact, the electrical path can go from one arm across the heart to the other arm. If only one hand is used, it goes from the arm down a leg to the ground.

(0.025 A) may be fatal, you realize that even circuits with 0.5-A protection devices have the potential to be lethal—never mind 15- or 20-A protected circuits. Fuses and circuit breakers do *not* provide the level of safety against shock and electrocution that many people believe they do. Figures 3 and 4 show typical fuses and circuit breakers.

Overhead wires

When working in areas with overhead power lines, you must exercise caution to maintain a safe and clear distance from these wires. Voltages in many overhead power lines exceed those that most HVACR technicians normally deal with—and therefore, standard personal protective equipment (PPE) may not be sufficient. Working around high voltages and currents requires specialized training in detailed procedures, suitable PPE, appropriately rated ladders, and approved equipment.

Technicians often may find themselves in situations where cranes are present. Extreme care must be exercised to prevent the crane boom or cables from coming close to or touching live power lines. In many cases, the wires are bare and represent a high level of danger not only to the crane operator, but also to anyone else on the crane or in contact with conductive materials through which current may travel.

Exposed wiring

Exposed wiring, loose terminals, poorly insulated connectors, uncovered panels and electrical boxes, stripped or nicked insulation, improperly tightened or installed wire connectors, poor or missing wire markings, and frayed cords are all potential sources of electric shock. Prior to opening a panel or equipment access door, perform a visual inspection to verify the integrity of the wiring entering the panel. Loose connectors, exposed wires,

COOPER BUSSMANN, INC.

▲ *Figure 3* Typical time-delay fuses

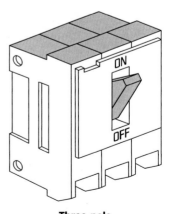

◄ *Figure 4* Typical circuit breakers

Single-pole   **Two-pole**   **Three-pole**

incorrect conduit type, and water stains on the exterior should be regarded as potential hazards and treated appropriately by using the necessary PPE. *Always* exercise extreme care when accessing an energized electrical panel for testing or servicing!

Overloaded circuits

Electric shock may occur when there are too many devices connected into a single circuit, or when the wiring is undersized for the current requirements, or when fuses or circuit breakers are rated too high for the wire size. In many such cases, the wiring may feel warm to the touch, and may even begin to melt before the overload protection device opens.

Circuits and the overload devices that protect them are designed and rated for a maximum amount of current draw. If the devices connected to the circuit draw more current than the circuit is rated for, an overload situation will occur. If the circuit is properly installed with the correct circuit protection (such as a fuse or a circuit breaker), the wiring and devices will not be damaged. In cases where fuses or circuit breakers are improperly sized—usually oversized for the circuit wiring—the potential for a wiring "meltdown" leading to a fire exists. Remember that this is the function of fuses and circuit breakers—to prevent overcurrent situations from happening.

A common example of overloaded circuits often occurs during holiday seasons when decorative lights are used to decorate a home. In many cases, fires during the holiday seasons are attributed to overloaded electric circuits. Also, the use of too many power tools or tools with high current draws on a common circuit (single extension) cord may cause the premature failure of the wiring and the tools, possibly leading to shocks and other related injuries.

Never overload electric lines. Consult your local electrical code, or the U.S. or Canadian electrical codes, as to permissible wattage and current for various sizes and types of wires. Refuse to install equipment that will add loads above allowable limits. Use only properly sized fuses and overload devices. *Never* bypass them.

Improper grounding

All electrical systems and equipment must have some type of grounding protection to help prevent the unintentional energizing of any metal components within the system, including boxes, switches, motors, and casings. The grounding system should be at 0 Ω, allowing the current a safe path of least resistance in case any part or component of the system becomes energized.

▶ SAFETY TIP ◀

Warning: Electrical work can be shocking

Proper equipment and procedures are necessary when checking voltage supplies. Do not attempt to take measurements on high-voltage systems (600 V or more) with hand-held instruments. Always use current and potential transformers to make high-voltage measurements. Be sure that you ground all electrical equipment and discharge capacitors before touching them.

Don't work on electrical components until you are sure that all power is off and no residual voltage can leak from capacitors or solid-state components. When working on dead lines, be aware that induced voltage from adjacent lines can startle you. While the shock itself may not hurt you, a subsequent fall can. It's best to make sure that power is off to any adjacent circuit.

Don't tighten any connection on a terminal board until the main disconnect switch is off. Never try to stop a machine by opening an isolating knife switch, since high-intensity arcing can occur. Be aware that certain automatic start arrangements can engage the starter, and open the disconnect ahead of the starter in addition to shutting off the machine or pump.

SOURCE: EMPIRE KEYSTONE ASSOCIATION SAFETY HANDBOOK

Any and all metal components in an electrical system have the potential to provide an electric shock. Therefore, all electrical systems and components must be properly grounded in order to prevent a shock if physical contact is made. The purpose of a grounding circuit is to provide a safe path of least resistance for electrical faults, preventing exposed parts and components from becoming energized. Damaged plugs, loose connections, improperly connected wiring, and missing, broken, or damaged wiring insulation all can cause an electric shock if equipment is not properly grounded.

Water piping is to be grounded to an exterior conductive rod driven into the ground. If this is not done properly and the piping becomes energized, taps and faucets also could become energized, causing severe electric shocks. Gas piping is to be "bonded" (jumper-wired) to water piping or any other direct grounding source to prevent all gas appliances connected to the gas piping from becoming energized.

Unfortunately, one of the most common errors that careless technicians (and others) make is the use of cords and equipment from which the grounding prong has been broken off or removed. This prevents the grounding circuit from forming a complete path for the current, leaving equipment, tools, metal conductors, and components energized.

Wet conditions

Wet conditions due to high humidity levels, rain, standing water, damp floors, perspiration, etc., reduce the resistance of normal dry skin and clothing, thus allowing a path for current to travel. In wet conditions, the risk of receiving an electric shock from damaged tools, poorly maintained extension cords, damaged wiring insulation, or bare wires and terminals is greatly increased.

Always check the integrity of the insulation of tools and wiring. Look for nicks, cuts, abrasions, and cracks prior to use to reduce the chances of shock. Remember that current always takes the path of least resistance—and in wet conditions or moist atmospheres, that path may be *through* the moisture and *through* the parts of your body that are in contact with the tool. Use waterproof wires and connectors, locking plugs, double-insulated tools, and insulated gloves to guard against shocks when working in wet conditions. Using uninsulated tools in these circumstances is extremely dangerous!

GROUND-FAULT CIRCUIT INTERRUPTERS

A *ground-fault circuit interrupter* (GFCI) is a device that disconnects the load from the power source when activated by an imbalance between the

▶ SAFETY TIP ◀

Don't give electricity an "opening"

The GFCI is a fast-acting circuit breaker that senses small imbalances in a circuit caused by current leakage to the ground and—in a fraction of a second—shuts off electricity. This prevents electrocution and protects against fires, overheating, and damage to wiring insulation.

Normally, GFCI receptacles (like those found in a bathroom) can sense ground-fault circuits. However, if the line-side neutral conductor is opened or lifted at a panel, the circuitry in the GFCI receptacle will not have the necessary 125-V power from which to operate. This means that the GFCI is no longer capable of sensing or disengaging, which is termed as "open neutral." An open neutral also is known as a "no voltage" or "dropped voltage" feature.

If a technician connects a faulty tool to a receptacle without open neutral protection, he or she will be exposed to a shock or electrocution hazard. This is why job site GFCIs must provide open neutral protection. Open neutral protection occurs when both the hot and neutral circuits on the load side of the GFCI are opened (or disengaged) in the event the neutral or hot wires on the line side of the GFCI are opened.

SOURCE: ERICSON MANUFACTURING COMPANY

line current and the neutral current. These devices are commonly found in exterior wall plugs and in other areas where there is a potential risk of moisture, such as bathrooms and laundry rooms. The presence of moisture in the vicinity of electrical equipment drastically decreases resistances—and increases the likelihood of electric shock. Installing a GFCI greatly reduces your chances of receiving an electric shock. It takes only a very small current imbalance (3 to 5 mA), present for a fraction of a second, to trip a GFCI.

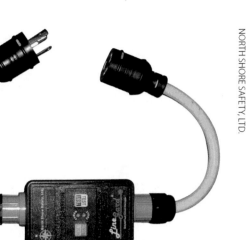

▲ *Figure 5* Portable GFCI

Normally, GFCIs are permanently installed in wall sockets, but they are also available for electrical panels and for portable (temporary) applications. HVACR technicians who utilize portable electric tools are advised to make use of a portable GFCI to help reduce the chances of electric shock (see Figure 5). Doing so provides an added safeguard that makes good sense, especially under the adverse outdoor conditions to which technicians may be exposed.

In order for a permanent GFCI to function correctly, it is important that the device be installed per the manufacturer's instructions. An improperly installed GFCI offers no protection against electric shock. In many applications, a GFCI is installed in the main electrical panel as part of the circuit breaker, providing added protection against shocks from the entire electric circuit (see Figure 6).

PERSONAL PROTECTIVE EQUIPMENT

The use of PPE when troubleshooting electrical equipment is too often ignored. When was the last time you noticed an HVACR technician using insulated gloves, protective eyewear, a face shield, insulated work boots, or insulated clothing when checking the power on an air conditioning, refrigeration, or heating unit control panel? Sadly, it is routine for many technicians *not* to wear any PPE. However, many occurrences of electric shocks and related injuries could be prevented by using the proper PPE.

Electrical codes are becoming more and more stringent regarding the mandatory use of PPE. Codes are also addressing various types of meters and the training required for working around electric circuits—including low-voltage systems with voltage supplies of less than 30 V ac.

▲ *Figure 6* Panel-mount utility GFCI

Once you have begun using PPE, it is important to check your equipment regularly, as manufacturers and codes require, ensuring that it has not been damaged or degraded due to the passage of time or poor storage conditions. Always follow a set procedure, which includes selecting appropriate PPE for the task at hand, inspecting it thoroughly, and using it properly. Doing so can save a life!

NFPA 70E: ELECTRICAL SAFETY IN THE WORKPLACE

The National Fire Protection Association (NFPA) establishes electrical safety requirements for the workplace in Standard 70E. The standard requires that equipment operating at 50 V or more be de-energized (in most cases, through a proper lockout/tagout procedure) before any work is done on the piece of equipment. The standard acknowledges that there are certain tasks—such as testing voltages and other troubleshooting procedures—that cannot be done unless the equipment is energized. The standard requires that PPE be used to protect the worker from three potential hazards: electric shock, arc-flash, and arc-blast, defined as follows:

▶ **Electric shock.** An uninsulated part of the body makes contact with an energized electric circuit.

▶ **Arc-flash.** Intense heat and light energy are generated by an electrical short circuit condition.

▶ **Arc-blast.** An explosion, which may include flying parts and molten metal, results from the rapidly expanding gas generated by a short circuit condition.

The greatest potential hazards for arc-flash and arc-blast in a building exist at the main panel boards, switch boards, and motor control centers.

NFPA 70E divides different types of work into different hazard categories. The examples listed below are intended as a general summary and are not meant to be all-inclusive:

▶ **Class 0—minimal risk.** Circuit breaker and switch operations with the covers closed.

▶ **Class 1—some risk.** Circuit breaker and switch operations with the covers open, working on panel boards with 240 V or less, opening covers exposing energized parts at 277 to 600 V.

▶ **Class 2—moderate risk.** Circuit breaker and switch operations above 600 V, working on energized 120-V control circuits.

▶ **Class 3—high risk.** Insertion or removal of circuit breakers, opening panels or switchgear at 600 V and above.

▶ **Class 4—greatest risk.** Working on 2,300 to 7,200-V transformers above 1,000 V.

Voltage testing on equipment at less than 240 V typically requires a long-sleeved fire-resistant shirt, cotton pants, voltage-rated gloves, safety glasses, and a hard hat. At higher voltages, an arc-flash hazard assessment needs to be done to determine proper PPE.

▼ *Figure 7* Typical digital multimeter

METER SAFETY

Electrical meters are so commonly used by service technicians that most take them for granted. Rarely are meters considered a source of potential danger. But the electrical meter, being as versatile and easy to use as it is, can very easily become the path of current between the power supply and the technician!

In most cases, the voltage supply for HVACR equipment does not exceed 600 V. For such applications, it is important to use a meter with a Category III 1,000-V rating minimum. This rating means that the meter has the proper circuit protection (fusing) and insulating leads to be used safely in most HVACR applications. Figure 7 shows a typical digital multimeter.

Even with the safety features built into your electrical meter and test leads, an electrical meter, if improperly used, still has the potential to explode! All meters have a power source (a battery), which always has the potential to explode. This may occur if the meter selector switch is moved from scale to scale while connected to a power source, or if the power source exceeds the rated value of the meter, or if a circuit is not properly isolated between various measurements.

LOCKOUT/TAGOUT PROGRAMS

It is critical that every employer establish a lockout/tagout (LOTO) program and that every employee be aware of the LOTO procedures for ensuring that equipment being installed, maintained, inspected, or serviced does not become energized unintentionally. Note that the word "accidentally" is not used in this case. Why? Because the energizing of an electrical source while an individual is working on it is *absolutely unacceptable* and *completely avoidable*, provided a proper LOTO program is in place and the required procedures are followed.

All employees must use individualized locks and tags. The tags notify others that work is being performed on a certain system, and the locks prevent anyone else from energizing the system without authorization from the individual who has isolated the system for safety purposes. All too often, individuals are injured or killed due to the fact that LOTO procedures have not been established or have not been followed properly. Figure 8 shows an assortment of LOTO hasps, tags, and padlocks.

Injuries and deaths attributable to electric shock can be avoided by a comprehensive LOTO program, complete with periodic safety training, clearly written procedures, and proper lockout/tagout equipment. For a full description of a LOTO program, view the material available from the Environmental Safety and Health Group of OSHA at www.osha.gov.

Requiring employee awareness training, following detailed procedures, observing safe practices, using proper PPE—these are things that save lives when dealing with electrical systems, regardless of the type of equipment or voltage supply. Make full use of the knowledge you have gained and the safety skills you have developed to prevent even the smallest of electric shocks—the next one you receive could be your last! ■

▲ **Figure 8** Lockout/tagout items

IDEAL INDUSTRIES, INC.

Fan Safety

Fans and other air-moving devices are made in a wide variety of types, sizes, and arrangements. Properly installed and used, they help create a better environment for human comfort—both indoors and outdoors. Improperly used or installed, they become a potential danger to life and limb. Caution should be used at all times when working in or around moving parts.

This Chapter is intended to assist in the safe installation and maintenance of air-moving equipment and to warn operating and maintenance personnel of some of the hazards associated with this equipment. *Installation should always be performed only by experienced and trained personnel.* In addition to following the manufacturer's installation instructions, technicians must be careful to ensure compliance with federal, state, and local government requirements.

PERSONNEL SAFETY ACCESSORIES

Protective devices are incorporated as standard equipment on some types of fans, but on many fans these devices are offered as optional accessories. This is done because the need for the devices and the design required is dependent on the type of system, fan location, and operating procedures being employed. The proper protective safety device to meet company standards, local codes, and OSHA requirements must be determined by the user, since safety requirements vary depending on the location of the equipment. The user should specify and obtain appropriate protective safety devices from the fan manufacturer or others, and should not allow the operation of the equipment without them.

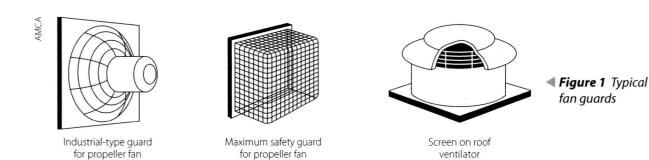

| Industrial-type guard for propeller fan | Maximum safety guard for propeller fan | Screen on roof ventilator |

◀ *Figure 1* *Typical fan guards*

FAN GUARDS

All fans have moving parts that require guarding in the same way as other moving machinery (see Figure 1). In areas that are accessible only to experienced and trained personnel, a standard industrial-type guard may be adequate. This type of guard will provide protection against thrown or dropped objects with the minimum restriction of air flow.

Where the fan is accessible to untrained personnel or the general public, maximum safety guards should be used. Fans located less than 7 ft (2.1 m) above the floor require special consideration, as specified by OSHA. Even roof-mounted equipment requires guards when access is possible, for example, by climbing children.

Inlet and outlet guards

Axial and centrifugal fans are usually connected directly to ductwork, which will prevent contact with the internal moving parts. When the inlet or outlet is exposed, a suitable guard should be installed (see Figure 2).

Drive guards

Fans may be driven directly from the motor shaft or through a belt drive. In every case where the bearing assembly, rotating shaft, sheaves, or belts are exposed, a suitable guard needs to be provided (see Figure 3). Even on

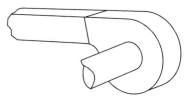

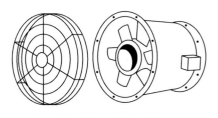

| Centrifugal fan protected by ductwork | Inlet or outlet guard on centrifugal fan | Guard for axial fan with non-ducted inlet or outlet |

▲ *Figure 2* *Inlet and outlet guards*

AMCA

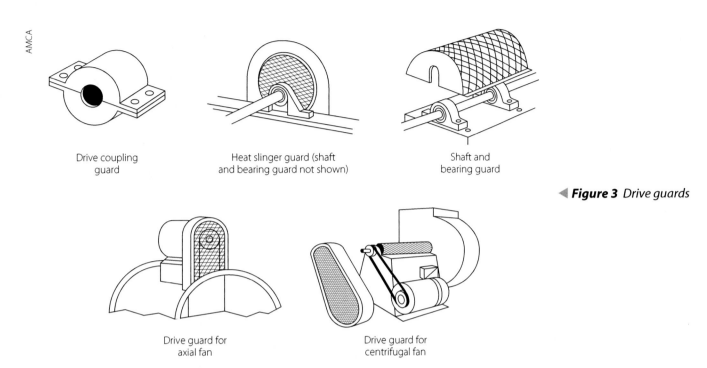

Drive coupling
guard

Heat slinger guard (shaft
and bearing guard not shown)

Shaft and
bearing guard

◀ *Figure 3* Drive guards

Drive guard for
axial fan

Drive guard for
centrifugal fan

tubular or axial fans, where only part of the drive is exposed, a partial guard
should be installed.

In restricted access areas, one-sided guards of expanded metal may be
acceptable. Readily accessible locations require maximum protection guards
and even, in some cases, a fully enclosed sheet metal guard.

HIDDEN DANGERS

In addition to the obvious hazards associated with the moving parts of
rotating machinery, a fan presents another potential hazard in its ability
to "suck in" loose material. Solid objects can pass through the fan and be
discharged by the wheel as potentially dangerous projectiles.

Intakes to ductwork should, whenever possible, be screened to prevent the
accidental entrance of solid objects. A system that handles sawdust, for
example, should be equipped with an intake screen that will allow the
entry of sawdust but prevent the entry of chunks of wood (see Figure 4).

Fan design sometimes requires special access doors to be installed in the
ductwork (see Figure 5 on the next page). *The access doors to a duct system
should never be opened when the fan if running.* On the downstream (or
pressure) side of the system, releasing the door with the system in operation
may result in an explosive opening. On the upstream (or suction) side, the

▼ *Figure 4* Special-purpose
intake screen

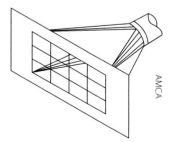

AMCA

inflow may be sufficient to suck in tools, clothing, and small objects, and may even cause a person to lose his or her balance. Quick-release handles should *not* be provided on access doors, since they are a potential hazard.

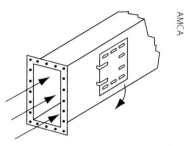

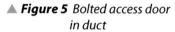

▲ **Figure 5** *Bolted access door in duct*

START-UP CHECK LIST

Before putting any fan into operation for the first time, carefully complete the following checklist:

1. Lock out the primary and all secondary power sources.
2. Perform a complete inspection of all of the ductwork and the interior of the fan. Make certain there is no foreign material that can be drawn into or blown through the fan or ductwork.
3. Make sure the foundation or mounting arrangement and the duct connections are adequately designed in accordance with recognized acceptable engineering practices and with the fan manufacturer's recommendations.
4. Check and tighten all hold-down (securing) bolts.
5. Spin the wheel to see if it rotates freely, without binding or rubbing. Inspect the wheel to see if it is the proper rotation for the fan design.
6. Check all set screws and tighten, if necessary.
7. Check the V-drive or coupling for alignment. Use the recommended belt tension.
8. Check the V-drive for proper sheave selection. Make sure that the sheaves are not reversed—if they are, the fan may run at excessive speeds.
9. Properly secure all safety guards.
10. Secure all access doors to the fan and ductwork.
11. Switch on the electrical supply and allow the fan to reach full speed. Then check carefully for:
    a. correct wheel rotation
    b. excessive vibration
    c. unusual noise
    d. proper belt alignment
    e. proper lubrication
    f. proper current and voltage values.

If any problem is indicated, *switch off the power immediately.* Lock out the electrical supply, check carefully for the cause of the trouble, and correct as necessary.

Even if the fan appears to be operating satisfactorily, it is a good idea to shut down the system after a brief period and recheck items 3 through 11. The initial start-up may have loosened bolts and set screws.

The fan may now be put into operation but, during the first eight hours of running, it should be periodically observed and checked for excessive vibration and noise. At this time, checks should also be made of motor input current and motor and bearing temperatures to ensure that they do not exceed the manufacturer's recommendations.

After eight hours of satisfactory operation, the fan should be shut down and the power locked out to check (and, if necessary, to adjust) the following:
- all set screws and hold-down bolts
- the drive coupling alignment
- the V-drive alignment.

After 24 hours of operation, the fan should be shut down and the V-drive belt should be readjusted to the recommended tension.

ELECTRICAL ISOLATION

Every fan must be provided with a disconnect switch that will allow it to be isolated completely from the electrical supply.

Most roof-mounted fans (and many others) are started by remote switches or pushbuttons, by interlocks with other equipment, or by automatic controls. In such cases, a disconnect switch must be provided close to the fan so that maintenance personnel can "positively" cut off the power when working on the fan.

In some installations other equipment, such as gas burners, may be interlocked with the fan, so that disconnecting the fan will automatically shut off the burner or other device. Maintenance on systems of this type should be performed only under the supervision of competent service personnel.

SPECIAL-PURPOSE SYSTEMS

Fans that are used to move anything other than clean air at normal temperatures (say, up to 150°F) may require special precautions to ensure safe operation. The hazards inherent in systems in which explosive or toxic fumes or gases, transported solids, high temperatures, or corrosive contaminants are present must be carefully considered. All federal, state, and local codes should be reviewed, together with any applicable industry standards. The fan manufacturer's recommendations for the specific type of application also should be closely followed.

In systems that handle explosive or inflammable fumes or gases, fans of spark-resistant construction should be used. AMCA Standard 401-96

▶ **SAFETY TIP** ◀

Working in fan plenums requires caution and care

Fan plenums usually are dimly lit and have little extra room. They also have moving parts, such as V-belt drives. Working in and around fan plenums requires special precautions. Here are a few:

▷ Let someone know you are entering a plenum in case you get trapped.
▷ Do not wear loose clothing or long sleeves that can catch on moving parts.
▷ If you have long hair, tie it up or tuck it beneath a cap.
▷ Carry a flashlight to use in dimly lit areas.
▷ Before entering, look for places where you could possibly hit your head, such as light-bulb covers.
▷ Carry a cordless phone, especially if working alone.
▷ Always open the fan plenum doors carefully. Excess pressure can blow doors open violently on the fan discharge side.
▷ Be aware that if outside and return-air dampers close, negative pressure can prevent you from opening the plenum door.
▷ Before entering, remove all debris and stored material, since it increases the chances of tripping.

SOURCE: LAMA BOOKS, SAFETY FOR THE INDOOR ENVIRONMENT TECHNICIAN

defines the industry's standard types of spark-resistant construction and should be consulted when specifying fans for this use.

If the fan is handling toxic or explosive fumes—even in traces—care must be taken to ensure that fumes do not collect in areas accessed by service personnel. Concentrations of fumes can collect in "air trap" areas, particularly when a system is shut down.

Material-handling fans are specially designed to allow the fan to handle a specific type of material without excessive accumulation of material on the fan wheel. To ensure satisfactory operation, it is essential to observe the manufacturer's limitations concerning the type of material to be handled by the fan.

Fan ratings and maximum speed limits are typically based on the use of air at 70°F. At temperatures above the normal range (i.e., above 150°F), a reduction must be made in the maximum speed limit. Information on this reduction and on other precautions to be taken for high-temperature applications should be obtained from the fan manufacturer.

Corrosive contaminants can be formed when moisture combines with an active airborne chemical. Unprotected fans subjected to corrosive contaminants will eventually fail, but suitable construction materials or protective coatings can resist corrosion. Even fans protected with special coatings must be inspected regularly to ensure that the protection remains effective.

In outdoor installations where water can accumulate within the fan housing, provide for the installation of adequately sized drain plugs.

ROUTINE MAINTENANCE

Do not attempt any maintenance on a fan unless the electrical supply has been completely disconnected. If a disconnect switch has not been provided, remove all fuses from the circuit and lock the fuse panel so that they cannot be replaced.

Under normal circumstances, handling clean air, the system will require cleaning only about once a year. However, the fan and system should be checked at regular intervals to detect any unusual accumulation.

The fan wheel should be specially checked for build-up of material or dirt, which may cause an imbalance with resulting undue wear on bearings and

---

▶ **SAFETY TIP** ◀

Servicing air-handling equipment safely

Air-handling equipment will provide safe and reliable service when operated within design specifications. When operating or servicing this equipment, use good judgment and safe practices to avoid injury or damage to equipment or property:

▷ Never enter an enclosed fan cabinet or reach into a unit while the fan is running.

▷ Lock out and tag out the fan motor power disconnect switch before working on a fan. In addition, remove the fuses and take them with you after noting this on the tag.

▷ Lock out and tag out the power disconnect switch of the electric heat coil before working on or near heaters.

▷ Don't operate fans unless belt guards are in place.

▷ Never pressurize a coil with a nonliquid to leak test. A dangerous burst may occur.

▷ Don't steam clean coils until you are sure that all personnel are clear of the area. Wear safety goggles during steam cleaning, high-pressure water cleaning, and compressed air cleaning activities.

▷ Check to ensure that there is adequate ventilation when welding or flamecutting inside an air-handling unit so that fumes will not migrate through the ductwork to occupied spaces.

(continued next page)

V-belt drives. A regular maintenance program should be established as needed to prevent this build-up.

Regular inspection of the rotating assembly should be made to detect any indication of weakening of the rotor due to corrosion, erosion, or metal fatigue.

Excessive vibration

Check for material build-up on the wheel. Generally this will show up as material flaking off the fan wheel and causing an imbalance that may lead to fatigue failure. Never allow a fan to operate if the amplitude of vibration is above the maximum safe limit. Contact the fan manufacturer for this information if it is not included in maintenance instructions.

High motor temperatures

Check that cooling air to the motor has not been diverted or blocked by dirty guards or similar obstacles. Check the input current. An increase in power may indicate that some major change has occurred in the system.

High bearing temperatures

This condition is usually caused by improper lubrication (either "over" or "under"). In every case, if the cause of the trouble is not easily seen, experienced personnel should examine the equipment before it is put back in operation.

CONCLUSION

A preventive maintenance program is an important aspect of an effective safety program. *Maintenance should always be performed by experienced and trained personnel who are aware of the hazards associated with rotating equipment.* Maintenance records that keep track of inspection and repair history should be maintained and consulted during the scheduled program inspection. Maintenance logs should contain a complete history of repairs made and measurements taken, including among other things:

- lubrication
- vibration levels
- temperature levels
- power requirements.

Any abnormalities should be noted and addressed as soon as possible.

Note: Portions of this Chapter were prepared by the Air Movement Division of the Air Movement and Control Association, Inc. (AMCA). ■

(continued from previous page)

▷ Do not handle access covers and removable panels where winds are strong or gusting unless you have sufficient help to control them. Make sure that all panels are properly secured while repairs are being made to a unit.

▷ Do not work on dampers until you have disconnected their operators.

▷ Check to be sure that fans and rooftop units are properly grounded, locked out, and tagged out before working on them.

▷ Secure drive sheaves with rope or strap before working on a fan to be sure that the fan does not freewheel.

▷ Protect adjacent flammable material when welding or flamecutting. Use sheet metal or flame-retardant cloth to contain sparks. Have a fire extinguisher at hand and ready for immediate use.

▷ Never pressurize equipment in excess of specified test pressures.

Refrigerants and Other Gases

Using a refrigerant to move heat from one area to another appears to be a simple matter, but understanding *how* a refrigerant transfers heat is much more difficult. In many applications, due to the complexity of the various systems in which refrigerants are expected to perform, one of the most important factors regarding refrigerants gets buried or forgotten in all the technical content—and that is safety.

Most technicians naturally prefer to work with nontoxic, nonflammable, and nonexplosive refrigerants, but this is not always possible. This Chapter puts the emphasis on the *properties* of refrigerants, rather than on their technical applications and uses, in order to help you gain a better understanding of how to be safe when handling refrigerants.

REFRIGERANT PROPERTIES

Let's briefly review some of the properties that make various refrigerants desirable for use in refrigeration and air conditioning systems—and also raise questions about how to handle them properly.

Boiling point

Because the boiling points of refrigerants can vary from a hundred degrees or more below 32°F (0°C) to a hundred degrees or more above 32°F (0°C), safety becomes an obvious concern. Consider the case of water, which has a boiling point of 212°F (100°C) at atmospheric pressure. People instinctively understand the consequences of being exposed to water at this temperature. Exposure to water at a temperature of 32°F (0°C) has consequences of a different nature, but both extremes can be dangerous. The point is that knowing the expected boiling point of a refrigerant at a typical working pressure (as well as at atmospheric pressure) will give you an indication of the severity of harm that can be caused.

For example, R-22 has a boiling point of approximately –40°F (–40°C) at atmospheric pressure. Direct exposure to the skin at this temperature—as a liquid or a vapor—can cause severe frostbite. Even worse, direct contact with the eyes may cause eye damage or blindness. Obviously, the severity and extent of the damage depend not only on the temperature of the refrigerant, but also on the amount of refrigerant to which you are exposed and the length of time for which you are exposed.

You may think that this is not likely to happen, but accidents can occur very easily—there may be an unexpected leak or line rupture, for example, when you are performing normal service, installation, or maintenance of equipment. Even under "everyday" conditions, exposure to skin and eyes may occur while you are carrying out a routine task like accessing a system with hoses and gauges at a pressure port. And don't forget that as the refrigerant pressure decreases, the refrigerant temperature also decreases—which increases the potential risk. Conversely, if the refrigerant pressure increases, the refrigerant temperature also increases, which can lead to severe refrigerant burns. Beware—refrigerants have the ability both to burn and to cause frostbite!

Table 1 shows a list of some common refrigerants and their boiling points at atmospheric pressure.

Stability

Under normal (clean and dry) conditions, the stability of a refrigerant is not a concern. However, if the refrigerant is exposed to contaminants such as water, air, or non-condensibles, or if it is subjected to excessive temperatures and pressures, refrigerant stability can become a safety issue.

Excessive temperatures within a refrigeration or air conditioning system may cause the refrigerant to decompose, leading to the formation of acids. For example, fluorocarbon

▼ *Table 1* Refrigerant boiling points

Refrigerant	Boiling point	ASHRAE Standard 34 safety classification
R-11	75°F (24°C)	A1
R-12	–21°F (–29°C)	A1
R-22	–40°F (–40°C)	A1
R-123	82°F (28°C)	B1
R-134a	–16°F (–27°C)	A1
R-290 (propane)	–44°F (–42°C)	A3
R-404A	–51°F (–46°C)	A1
R-407C	–46°F (–43°C)	A1
R-410A	–61°F (–52°C)	A1
R-600a	11°F (–12°C)	A3
R-717 (ammonia)	–28°F (–33°C)	B2
R-718 (water)	212°F (100°C)	A1
R-1150	–155°F (–104°C)	A3

refrigerant vapors will decompose on contact with hot metal surfaces, such as heating elements or heat exchangers on fossil fuel furnaces. The flames from brazing torches, open burners, or halide leak detectors also will cause halogenated refrigerants to decompose. (The use of halide leak detectors is no longer recommended, and in many cases is prohibited.) Depending on the type of refrigerant, the acid gases that result from decomposition may include hydrochloric, hydrofluoric, and carbonyl halides, which can corrode the metal in equipment and the cotton in clothing. These toxic and irritating gases often have a sharp, pungent odor. If this odor is detected, all personnel should leave the area, and the area must be ventilated until the air is cleared before work in the area can resume. In some cases, the decomposition of a refrigerant produces gases that may be carcinogenic, possibly leading to immediate and/or future health issues.

Excessive temperatures also may cause excessive internal pressures, leading to premature leaks or ruptures and the unexpected release of refrigerant. Use a suitable leak detector or soap solution to locate leaks. All personnel should leave the area until the refrigerant vapor has been dispersed with forced-air ventilation.

Noncondensibles in a system also lead to higher pressures, which in turn may elevate refrigerant temperatures. Excessive pressures and temperatures may not be evident until the system is accessed through an access port with a gauge manifold. Always exercise *extreme caution* when accessing a system.

When it comes to moisture in a system, the maximum allowable moisture limits for most refrigerants are listed in parts per million (ppm). Therefore, what constitutes "excessive moisture" is in reality mere droplets (grams) of water. Table 2 shows the relationship between parts per million and grams. Since 100 grams equals approximately 3.5 ounces, note that even 1,000 ppm in 100 lb of refrigerant is equivalent to only 45.4 grams—or about 1.6 ounces! Why are such minute amounts of moisture considered excessive, and why is it so important to protect against them? Because they may lead to the *hydrolysis* or "breakdown" of a halogenated refrigerant, causing the refrigerant to form hydrochloric and/or hydrofluoric acids. These acids not only attack the metal and glass-based components of a system, but also are very corrosive to any exposed human body parts.

With the increasing use of synthetic lubricants (polyolesters specifically), excessive amounts of moisture in a system also can cause the *lubricant* to

▼ *Table 2* Grams of water at 68°F (20°C)

ppm H$_2$O	Pounds of refrigerant		
	10	50	100
10	0.05	0.23	0.5
30	0.14	0.68	1.4
50	0.23	1.1	2.3
100	0.45	2.3	4.5
250	0.12	5.8	11.3
500	0.23	11.3	22.7
1000	0.45	22.7	45.4

become acidic, corrosive, and toxic. This adds to the concerns of direct exposure to a refrigerant during the removal of the refrigerant from a system—the refrigerant now may be contaminated with additional acids from the lubricant.

Flammability and toxicity

The flammability and toxicity of numerous refrigerants have been determined under various test conditions and, as a result, have been assigned a "Safety Classification" designation. This designation, listed in the ANSI/ASHRAE Standard 34, is an excellent reference source for comparing the flammability and toxicity ratings of various refrigerants.

Flammability. Fluorocarbon refrigerants are not flammable or explosive. If a refrigeration system is clean and dry and operating under normal pressures and temperatures, flammability is not a concern. However, as previously mentioned, refrigerants under elevated pressures and temperatures may become unstable. Under such conditions, if oxygen (air) is introduced, the refrigerant may become flammable, combustible, and explosive. This is one of the reasons why all of the air must be removed before adding refrigerant to a system. *Never* pressure-test or leak-test a system with air or oxygen! Use *only* an inert gas such as nitrogen or carbon dioxide (CO_2).

ANSI/ASHRAE Standard 34 provides three categories of flammability as follows:
- ▶ *No flame*—not flammable in air at atmospheric pressure.
  Examples: R-22, R-134a, R-410A
- ▶ *Mild flame*—may be flammable in air at atmospheric pressure.
  Example: R-717 (ammonia)
- ▶ *High flame*—highly flammable in air at atmospheric pressure.
  Examples: R-290 (propane), R-600 (butane)

The base elements used to manufacture most halogenated and hydrocarbon refrigerants are methane, ethane, propane, butane, or one of the derivatives of these products, such as isobutane, propene, and numerous others. Knowing the composition of the refrigerants that you handle will help you determine if a given refrigerant may be flammable or combustible, and under what conditions it may become so.

When you are brazing, soldering, or welding refrigerant piping or components, it is important to remove all of the refrigerant from the system and to purge the system with an inert gas, such as nitrogen (N_2) or carbon dioxide (CO_2). Using a torch on a sealed system that contains refrigerant

---

▶ **SAFETY TIP** ◀

Be wary of dangers posed by refrigerants

Service technicians should be familiar with the hazards of working with any refrigerant, especially when it comes in contact with the body:
▷ **Ingestion.** If ingestion occurs, do not induce vomiting. Seek medical attention immediately.
▷ **Skin or eye contact.** As with all refrigerants, care should be taken to avoid liquid contact with skin or eyes. Frostbite can occur if the liquid undergoes direct expansion. Promptly flush eyes or skin with lukewarm water. Seek medical attention. Polyolester (POE) oils also can cause skin irritations. Use appropriate gloves and safety glasses when handling POE lubricants.
▷ **Inhalation.** Inhaling high concentrations of refrigerant vapors first attacks the central nervous system, creating a narcotic effect. You also may experience a feeling of intoxication and dizziness with loss of coordination and slurred speech or symptoms. Cardiac irregularities, loss of consciousness and, ultimately, death can result from breathing this concentration. If any of these symptoms becomes evident, move to fresh air and seek immediate medical help.

SOURCE: UNIVERSAL R-410A SAFETY AND TRAINING, AC&R SAFETY COALITION

may cause an overpressurization of the system, creating the potential for the system piping or one of the components to rupture unexpectedly, releasing large amounts of refrigerant.

Nitrogen seems to be the inert gas of choice for purging—it is relatively inexpensive, easily obtainable, safely transported, contains no contaminants, and is recommended by most equipment manufacturers. Allowing a constant flow of inert gas through the system eliminates—or at least reduces—the possibility of igniting any refrigerant vapor that may not have been removed. The continuous flow of inert gas also reduces the risk of the lubricant igniting and burning, as well as the creation of any undesirable contaminants.

If a mixture of air and refrigerant is present in the system in the correct proportions, especially in a sealed system, the flame from a torch may cause the mixture to ignite within the system, causing an explosion. Exposure of refrigerants to open flames and high temperatures also may cause the refrigerant to decompose, which may lead to the production of toxic and irritating gases.

As you can see, there are numerous reasons for removing the entire refrigerant charge before using a torch on a system. To be on the safe side, always remove components or piping by cutting them out with a tube cutter, rather than by unsweating (de-brazing) the connection or components with a torch. The use of an open flame near any highly flammable refrigerant or lubricant could prove to be very hazardous to your health!

Toxicity. ANSI/ASHRAE Standard 34 classifies the toxicity of a refrigerant into two categories as follows:
- ▶ *Low toxicity*—equal to and above 400 parts per million (ppm).
  Examples: R-22, R-290 (propane), R-134a, R-410A
- ▶ *High toxicity*—equal to and below 399 parts per million (ppm).
  Examples: R-123, R-717 (ammonia)

These toxicity levels are applied to uncontaminated and non-decomposed refrigerants—basically, virgin refrigerants. Other products that may be introduced, such as lubricants, acids, or noncondensibles, are not included or measured for their combined toxicity levels.

A refrigerant's *acceptable exposure limit* (AEL) refers to the maximum recommended amount of time for which an individual can be exposed to the refrigerant (via inhalation) without suffering adverse effects. In most cases, this limit is set for an 8-hour period on a continuous basis, known as the *time-weighted average* (TWA). Extended exposure times beyond permissible TWA values may require the use of special breathing equipment to be safe.

Exposure to high concentration levels of a refrigerant may produce some or all of the following effects, depending on the concentration level, duration of exposure, and refrigerant type:

▶ nervous system depression
▶ anesthetic effects (insensitivity to pain)
▶ dizziness/drowsiness
▶ loss of coordination
▶ breathing difficulties
▶ unconsciousness
▶ cardiac irregularities
▶ cardiac arrest
▶ unexpected/unknown long-term effects
▶ death.

Another concern of handling refrigerants is that they have the ability to displace the air in a confined space such as an attic, equipment room, mechanical room, or service vehicle. Fluorocarbon refrigerant vapors are several times heavier than air, which means that areas where high concentrations may accumulate and displace oxygen must be well-ventilated before you enter. The issues of flammability and toxicity remain, but the obvious concern in this regard is the lack of oxygen to breathe. That is why it is so important to be aware of your surroundings and escape routes, especially when you are working in a confined space.

Because refrigerants present many potential risks, make it a habit to refer to manufacturer-provided safety literature, as well as to Material Safety Data Sheets (MSDSs), for up-to-date and pertinent safety information.

Although some refrigerants may have distinctive odors, *never* rely on your nose as your detection device. Many codes insist on the use of oxygen depletion sensors or refrigerant level monitors/alarms for various refrigerants. Become familiar with refrigerants that require these devices in your area. Also, be aware that special equipment (breathing apparatus) and training may be required when handling certain refrigerants in a variety of environments.

Personal protective equipment (PPE) to be used when handling refrigerants includes eyewear with side shields, impervious gloves, and protective clothing. Depending on their toxicity classifications, some refrigerants may require self-contained breathing apparatus when used in confined spaces or in mechanical rooms. When working around liquid refrigerant, make sure that your eyes and skin are protected from burns or frostbite. Again, familiarity with the characteristics and handling procedures of specific refrigerants is critical in staying safe. Make it your goal to learn more about the safety techniques required for handling the refrigerants you work with!

A final word of caution: Do not vent fluorocarbon refrigerants indoors or allow fluorocarbon liquids to run into floor drains. Always use proper recovery procedures when repairing or opening a sealed refrigeration system.

▼ **Figure 1** *Pressure-testing with dry nitrogen*

PRESSURE-TESTING

With the prohibition against venting refrigerants, as well as their rapidly rising cost, some service technicians may be tempted to pressure-test systems by using compressed air, with some refrigerant added, to permit the use of a refrigerant leak detector. This can be a hazardous practice. *Never* inject pure oxygen into a refrigeration system, and *never* heat any part of a refrigeration system containing refrigerant.

Observe the following safety guidelines when pressure-testing:
▶ Oxygen, or any combustible gas or combustible mixture of gases, must not be used to test for pressure or leaks, since such gases can react explosively with oil in the system.
▶ Never use the system compressor to build up pressure for testing.
▶ Use the proper refrigerant or gas for pressure-testing (that is, do not use fluorocarbons or carbon dioxide to test an ammonia system, or ammonia to test a fluorocarbon system).
▶ Take special care when using dry nitrogen for pressure-testing. The pressure in a nitrogen cylinder at room temperature is well above the bursting pressure of system components. For this reason, always use an approved nitrogen pressure-reducing valve or regulator between the cylinder and the system, in accordance with appropriate codes. Figure 1 shows an assembly with built-in relief valve.

SAFE HANDLING OF OTHER GASES

There are several other gases which, although not used as refrigerants, pose their own risks to HVACR service technicians in the field. Proper safety procedures must be followed in handling these gases. Misuse can result not only in major property damage, but also in serious injury or even death for the service technician and those in the immediate area.

Acetylene

This fuel gas, when burned in a simple torch that mixes the acetylene with air, gives a flame suitable for soft soldering, small silver-soldering and brazing, and other low heats (such as "lead burning," etc.). When burned in a torch that mixes the acetylene with oxygen, the flame is very hot, sufficient for heavy brazing, welding, and cutting.

Acetylene is, of course, highly flammable and must not be allowed to escape into a room, because a flame or an electric spark may ignite it. Make sure to follow the proper safety procedures and always wear the necessary PPE when using welding and brazing equipment that utilizes acetylene as the fuel gas.

Oxygen

Although oxygen itself is not flammable, it must be regarded and handled as being just as dangerous as a flammable gas, because it is the element that must be present (along with a flammable gas) to permit combustion.

Pure oxygen is dangerous in another way. It combines so rapidly with oils and other flammable materials that "spontaneous combustion" may occur—that is, the flammable material may burst into flame or explode without being ignited by a flame or spark.

 WARNING: *Never* allow oxygen to come in contact with oil. *Never* use oil on the fittings of an oxygen cylinder or a line. *Never* use oxygen to obtain a test pressure in any part of a refrigeration system, even though you may think that the system is free of oil. There may be a film of oil in the system that can cause spontaneous combustion or an explosion.

Hydrogen

Hydrogen in its gaseous state is colorless and tasteless. Its presence cannot be detected by the human senses. It is the lightest of all elements and diffuses rapidly through porous materials and through some metals at "red heat" (the temperature at which copper is bright red, just before it becomes molten). Hydrogen gas is flammable in air over a relatively wide range of mixtures (4 to 75%). It burns in air with a pale blue, almost invisible flame. When mixed in proper proportions with air, oxygen, or other oxidizers, it forms an explosive mixture. It is nontoxic, but can cause asphyxiation by the exclusion of breathable air (oxygen) in confined areas.

▶ **SAFETY TIP** ◀

Use respect, proper procedures when working with refrigerants

Fluorinated refrigerants must be treated with respect to avoid possible hazards associated with their use and handling. Heavy concentrations of a refrigerant within a confined area can displace enough oxygen to cause suffocation. Furthermore, if gas or electric burners are operating in the area, the refrigerant can decompose into hazardous substances.

High temperatures and, to a lesser degree, a combination of heat and water can cause refrigerants to break down into hydrofluoric and hydrochloric acids and an intermediate product, phosgene. If you detect a strong, irritating odor, warn others, leave the area immediately, and report it.

When working with refrigerants, remember these safety tips:
▷ Obtain a Material Safety Data Sheet (MSDS) for the specific refrigerant and follow the manufacturer's instructions.
▷ Do not enter or perform work inside any vessel without proper protection. This means that you must follow the confined space procedures set up by your company.
▷ Do not enter any equipment room or space containing air conditioning or refrigeration

(continued next page)

Liquid hydrogen is transparent and odorless. Its density is about ¼ that of water. It is not corrosive or significantly reactive. The low temperature of liquid hydrogen can solidify any gas except helium. With the exception of helium, all known substances are essentially insoluble in liquid hydrogen. Hydrogen reacts with air or oxygen only in the presence of a catalyst (e.g., platinum black) or a stimulus such as an arc, spark, or flame. It is hyperbolic with fluorine (it requires no source of ignition).

Hydrogen must be treated with the utmost care. It is an extremely flammable gas that is used quite extensively in factories and large shops instead of acetylene, since it produces a very hot flame when it is burned with oxygen. Hydrogen is also used as a refrigerant in ultra low-temperature applications such as cryogenics.

Carbon dioxide

Carbon dioxide (CO_2), in addition to being a refrigerant, is widely used by HVACR service technicians as a pressure gas for such common tasks as testing and blowing out coils and other parts. It is "inert" to practically all materials used in refrigerating equipment and makes a good gas for such purposes.

Carbon dioxide is composed of carbon and oxygen, but is entirely non-flammable. In fact, it is formed when carbon or other fuels (nearly all of which contain carbon) are burned. Carbon dioxide is frequently used in fire extinguishers and fire suppression systems, because it forms a "blanket" that deprives the fire of oxygen and smothers the flames.

Nitrogen

Nitrogen, which is the major constituent of air in the atmosphere (78% by volume, or 75% by mass), is produced by the distillation of liquid air. Liquid nitrogen is a clear, colorless, odorless, and tasteless fluid resembling water. It is only slightly soluble in water, and is a poor conductor of electricity and heat. As the main ingredient of air, nitrogen is mostly inert. It does not produce toxic or irritating vapors.

Nitrogen at room temperature and pressure does not react readily with other elements. It neither burns nor supports combustion. At elevated temperatures, it combines with some of the more active metals (such as calcium, sodium, and magnesium) to form nitrites. At high pressures and temperatures or in the presence of catalysts, a wide variety of compounds can be formed, among them ammonia, nitrous oxides, and complex carbon-metallic compounds.

(continued from previous page)

equipment after a known refrigerant spill until you are trained in confined space procedures.
▷ Avoid spilling liquid refrigerant on your skin or getting it into your eyes—always wear gloves and safety goggles. Wash any spills from the skin with soap and water. If any refrigerant enters your eyes, immediately flush your eyes with water and consult a physician.
▷ Do not weld or flame-cut any vessel or refrigerant line until the refrigerant has been removed.
▷ Avoid breathing refrigerant fumes and do not smoke in an atmosphere containing refrigerant vapor.

Refrigerants are heavier than air and will settle in all low places. Respiratory protection may be necessary for entry into and work within areas where a spill has occurred. Be sure that you are trained in your company's procedures for confined space entry and respirator use.

SOURCE: CARRIER SAFETY GUIDE FOR REFRIGERATION AND AIR-CONDITIONING EQUIPMENT

Nitrogen is used as a refrigerant in ultra low-temperature systems—that is, in the temperature range of $-344°F$ to $-260°F$ ($-209°C$ to $-162°C$).

Like carbon dioxide, nitrogen is an inert gas that is used for pressure-testing and blowing out coils. Nitrogen is also used in refrigeration system servicing and repair to purge air from tubing during welding and brazing operations, thus preventing oxidation of the interior walls of tubing. Only 3 to 5 psi of pressure is needed for the purging process. A commercial nitrogen cylinder contains approximately 2,500 psi of pressure at room temperature.

Ammonia

Anhydrous ammonia is a gas under atmospheric pressure, but is compressed to a liquid for handling. As a gas, it is lighter than air, and has a pungent, irritating odor readily identifiable at low concentrations. Voluntary exposure to dangerous concentrations is therefore unlikely. But prolonged exposure to even low concentrations should be avoided. Breathing ammonia vapor can damage the mucous membranes and lungs. Contact of liquid or vapor with skin or eyes can cause burns or blindness.

Ammonia vapor is flammable at high ignition temperatures within a very limited range of concentration, generally obtainable only under laboratory conditions.

All personnel working with anhydrous ammonia should be trained and experienced in its safe handling. That experience must include hazard recognition, the proper use of PPE, and first aid procedures required for ammonia refrigerants.

Before attempting maintenance or repair, make sure that all ammonia is removed from the system, including the compressor, condensers, receivers, and accumulators. Whenever possible, always stand upwind during any ammonia transfer operation, and utilize all proper personal protection equipment as required. ∎

Handling Cylinders Safely

Refrigerant cylinders are one of those things that too many technicians "take for granted"—they normally and automatically assume that the refrigerant cylinder carried up and down the ladder, in and out of the truck, across the hot roof, is not something that requires much thought or attention. The truth is exactly the opposite—refrigerant cylinders demand a great deal of respect, and are to be handled with extreme caution and care.

It's true that when refrigerant cylinders are properly handled, stored, and transported, they do what they are designed to do safely and reliably. But never allow yourself to become *too* confident or comfortable when working with refrigerant cylinders. Mishandling, misusing, or misapplying a refrigerant cylinder can lead to very dangerous situations!

REFRIGERANT CONTAINER CONSTRUCTION

A typical refrigerant cylinder is made of steel and welded together. It contains access valves or fittings and some type of relief device. The manufacturing, testing, and certification of cylinders are all designed to ensure a high level of safety.

Tanks

Tanks are typically used for bulk storage and delivery. They can be used to transport large quantities of refrigerants by truck or by railcar, and in many cases are fabricated on site. This type of container includes piping, pumps, motors, valves, gauges, and relief devices. Tanks are built and tested to American Society of Mechanical Engineers (ASME) pressure vessel code requirements and have nameplates indicating the necessary information.

Drums

Drums commonly used in the refrigeration industry tend to be of the nonrefillable, disposable type, and are used for lower-pressure refrigerants such as R-11, R-113, R-123, and others. These drums are classified as DOT (Department of Transportation) 17E and designed for single-trip use. Once empty, they must be disposed of properly. Reusable drums, which are also available, bear a DOT 5B classification.

Cylinders

Refrigerants usually are purchased and transported in cylinders. There is a variety of cylinder types and designs, which provide flexibility in size and quantity without sacrificing safety. The more common types of cylinders available include:

▶ **DOT 39.** These are single-trip, nonrefillable, disposable cylinders that have been used for decades for many refrigerants. They are appropriately rated for the type of refrigerant. *Note:* In many Canadian provinces, refrigerant in disposable (one-time use) cylinders may not be permitted.

▶ **DOT 4BA or DOT 4BW.** These are refillable, reusable, and recyclable. Used as recovery cylinders, they are becoming more and more common. Ratings must be appropriate for the refrigerant type—i.e., R-410A cylinders have higher pressure ratings than R-22 cylinders.

▶ **DOT 3AA.** These cylinders are used for refrigerants with higher pressure requirements—i.e., R-503, R-508, R-13, R-23.

▶ **DOT 110A.** These are nominal one-ton cylinders that contain approximately 1,700 to 2,000 lb of refrigerant, used for bulk delivery.

▼ *Figure 1* Recovery cylinder

Cylinder identification

The following paragraphs concentrate on refrigerant cylinders, because this is the type of container most frequently used in the field. However, much of the information also applies to other types of containers.

Markings. Every cylinder must provide certain information—typically stamped on the collar or handle—ensuring that the cylinder has met DOT or TC (Transport Canada) specifications and requirements. The following information normally is included:

▶ DOT or TC classification

▶ TW (tare weight)—the weight of the empty cylinder

▶ WC (water capacity)—the weight of water that the cylinder will hold at 60°F (15°C)

▶ date of manufacture or retest date

▶ manufacturer/owner

▶ pressure ratings.

Figure 1 shows an example of a recovery cylinder with a gray body and a yellow collar. The close-ups in Figure 2 are typical of the markings found on the collars of such cylinders.

Labels. Information applied to the cylinder in the form of labels normally includes the following:

▶ type of refrigerant
▶ net weight of the refrigerant
▶ color coding (ARI Guideline N)
▶ TDG (Transportation of Dangerous Goods) requirements
▶ bar coding
▶ MSDS (Material Safety Data Sheet) reference
▶ WHMIS (Workplace Health and Material Information System—Canada) reference.

Figure 3 is a facsimile of a warning label applied to a typical R-22 cylinder.

PRESSURE RATINGS

DOT regulations refer to two basic pressures—the *service* pressure and the *test* pressure. The DOT 39 is the most commonly used single-trip (disposable) cylinder for refrigerants such as R-22, R-134a, and R-401A. For example, a DOT 39 (260) cylinder has a service pressure of 260 psi and a test pressure of 325 psi. This is calculated using a 1.25 multiplier as set by DOT requirements (260 psi × 1.25 = 325 psi).

In the case of refrigerants like R-410A, the cylinder will have a DOT 39 (400) rating. This means that R-410A cylinders have a service pressure of 400 psi and a test pressure of 500 psi (400 psi × 1.25 = 500 psi) in order to contain the higher pressures exerted by this refrigerant. Table 1 on page 78 shows typical cylinder pressure ratings.

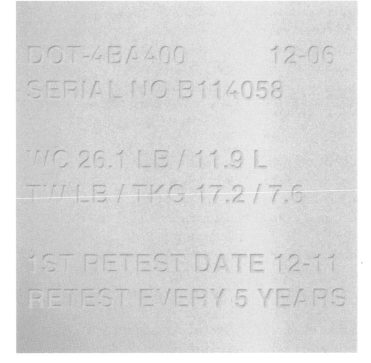

▲ *Figure 2* Typical cylinder markings

▲ *Figure 3* Typical cylinder label

In some cases you may notice a difference in the tare weight of cylinders with higher pressure ratings. This is because the material used to make the cylinder is thicker to withstand the greater internal pressures exerted by certain refrigerants.

ARI GUIDELINE N

ARI (Air Conditioning Institute) has developed a visual color-coding scheme for identifying refrigerant cylinders that has been adopted by most refrigerant manufacturers. This color coding not only makes identification easier and faster, it also makes the handling, storage, and transportation of a variety of refrigerants safer.

▼ **Table 1** *Typical cylinder pressure ratings (psi)*

Type of cylinder	Service pressure	Test pressure	Burst pressure	Relief device setting
DOT 39 (260)	260	325	650	341 to 520
DOT 39 (400)	400	500	1000	525 to 800
4BW or 4BA (260)	260	520	1040	390 to 800
4BW or 4BA (400)	400	800	1600	600 to 800
3AA (1800)	1800	2700	4050	2700 to 3000
110A (500)	333	500	1250	375 to 600

In the case of recovered/recycled refrigerant cylinders, the cylinder is white with a yellow top (head/collar/shoulder) identifying its application. Flammable refrigerants are marked with a red band on the top (head/collar/shoulder), making it easier to identify these refrigerants for proper handling, storage, and transportation.

Refrigerants are grouped into four classes, as follows:
▶ *Class I*—liquid refrigerants with a boiling point above 68°F (20°C), usually contained in drums
▶ *Class II*—low-pressure refrigerants with a cylinder service pressure below 260 psig (1793 kPa)
▶ *Class III*—high-pressure refrigerants with a cylinder service pressure above 260 psig (1793 kPa)
▶ *Class IV*—flammable refrigerants or mixtures that could become flammable in the event of a leak.

The color coding established by ARI follows what is referred to as the Pantone Matching System (PMS) for color matching, as shown in Figure 4.

CYLINDER SAFETY ISSUES

Accidents in which cylinders burst usually cause injury and/or death. It can only be assumed that in many cases the cylinders involved burst as a result of overfilling, overpressurization, misuse, or abuse. How can such accidents be avoided? One way is to be aware of—and pay attention to—safety guidelines set by manufacturers, DOT, and other authorities. In an effort to reduce

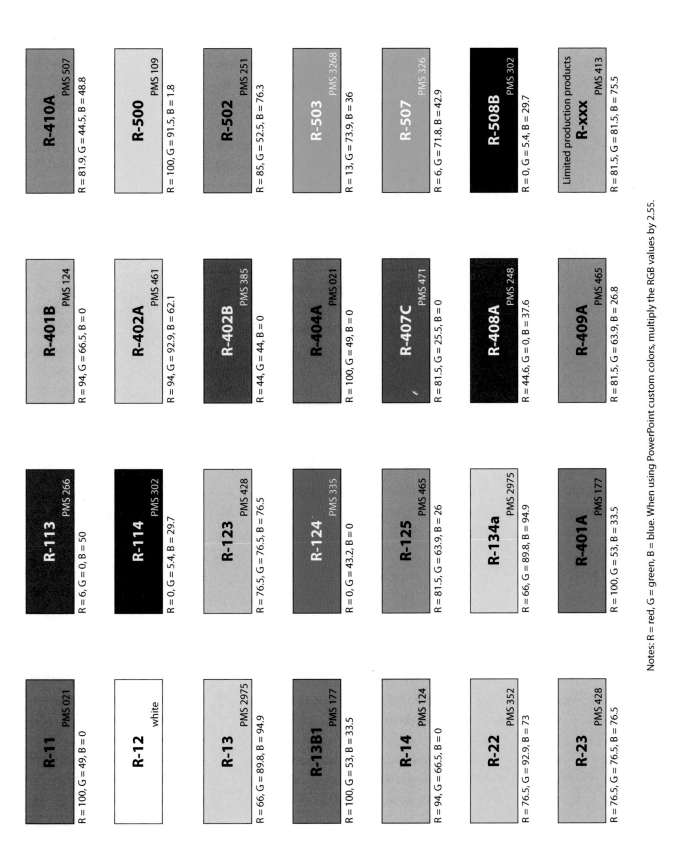

R-410A PMS 507
R = 81.9, G = 44.5, B = 48.8

R-500 PMS 109
R = 100, G = 91.5, B = 1.8

R-502 PMS 251
R = 85, G = 52.5, B = 76.3

R-503 PMS 3268
R = 13, G = 73.9, B = 36

R-507 PMS 326
R = 6, G = 71.8, B = 42.9

R-508B PMS 302
R = 0, G = 5.4, B = 29.7

Limited production products
R-xxx PMS 413
R = 81.5, G = 81.5, B = 75.5

R-401B PMS 124
R = 94, G = 66.5, B = 0

R-402A PMS 461
R = 94, G = 92.9, B = 62.1

R-402B PMS 385
R = 44, G = 44, B = 0

R-404A PMS 021
R = 100, G = 49, B = 0

R-407C PMS 471
R = 81.5, G = 25.5, B = 0

R-408A PMS 248
R = 44.6, G = 0, B = 37.6

R-409A PMS 465
R = 81.5, G = 63.9, B = 26.8

R-113 PMS 266
R = 6, G = 0, B = 50

R-114 PMS 302
R = 0, G = 5.4, B = 29.7

R-123 PMS 428
R = 76.5, G = 76.5, B = 76.5

R-124 PMS 335
R = 0, G = 43.2, B = 0

R-125 PMS 465
R = 81.5, G = 63.9, B = 26

R-134a PMS 2975
R = 66, G = 89.8, B = 94.9

R-401A PMS 177
R = 100, G = 53, B = 33.5

R-11 PMS 021
R = 100, G = 49, B = 0

R-12 white

R-13 PMS 2975
R = 66, G = 89.8, B = 94.9

R-13B1 PMS 177
R = 100, G = 53, B = 33.5

R-14 PMS 124
R = 94, G = 66.5, B = 0

R-22 PMS 352
R = 76.5, G = 92.9, B = 73

R-23 PMS 428
R = 76.5, G = 76.5, B = 76.5

Notes: R = red, G = green, B = blue. When using PowerPoint custom colors, multiply the RGB values by 2.55.

▲ **Figure 4** *ARI Guideline N (refrigerant cylinder colors and PMS numbers)*

the risk of such accidents, let's review some of the "basics." Here are four fundamental principles to keep in mind:

▶ As refrigerant cylinders are heated, the pressure increases, as does the liquid displacement of the refrigerant inside the cylinder.

▶ Once a cylinder is 100% full of liquid, a rapid rise in pressure occurs as a result of even a small increase in temperature. This is referred to as a *hydrostatic* condition.

▶ As refrigerants and noncondensable gases are mixed in a cylinder, the cylinder pressure rises according to the sum of the combined pressures (Dalton's Law).

▶ Misuse or abuse of the cylinder will reduce the cylinder's integrity (its ability to withstand the specified pressure ratings).

To understand these principles, think about what happens to the liquid refrigerant within a cylinder as heat is added or removed. You know that as the ambient temperature increases, the pressure inside the cylinder rises. As long as there is space for the expanding liquid to "move into," the cylinder will keep the liquid contained. However, if the temperature of the liquid continues to increase, eventually the liquid will no longer have space to "move into." At this point, because the cylinder cannot prevent the liquid refrigerant from expanding, the cylinder will quickly reach its burst pressure rating. Fortunately, cylinders have relief devices that should prevent this from happening. But if the hydrostatic pressure of the liquid increases faster than the relief device can relieve the pressure, there will be no other option for the cylinder but to burst. Also, if for some reason an incorrectly rated cylinder has been used—or if the relief device has been tampered with, or if the cylinder has been weakened due to damage or corrosion—then the relief device may not get the opportunity to perform as designed. All of these "ifs" can contribute to possible cylinder rupture.

Filling amounts

The previous paragraph explained that as the temperature of a refrigerant increases, the volume that the liquid refrigerant occupies or fills inside the cylinder also increases. This means that as the cylinder gets warmer, the amount of vapor space inside the cylinder decreases, allowing less space for the liquid to expand into. This fact is due to the *liquid density* of refrigerants. As the temperature of a liquid increases, the liquid density (pounds per cubic feet) decreases.

Typically, manufacturers fill a cylinder with liquid refrigerant according to the liquid density of the refrigerant at 130°F (54°C). This ensures that the cylinder holds a safe amount of refrigerant at the most extreme temperature

▶ **SAFETY TIP** ◀

Use safety, caution when handling refrigerants

The following is a list of do's and don'ts for handling refrigerants:

▷ Never use air to pressurize systems or vessels containing refrigerants for leak-testing or any other purpose.

▷ Never heat cylinders above 125°F (52°C). Do not place cylinders near flames or heat sources, or discard into fires.

▷ Never use torches or open flames to heat cylinders during refrigerant-charging operations.

▷ Never tamper with valves or pressure relief devices.

▷ Never refill disposable cylinders with anything. Any refrigerant remnants should be used or transferred to recovery containers, and the empty cylinder should be properly disposed of.

▷ Never refill disposable or returnable cylinders with reclaimed refrigerants or lubricants. Use only proper recovery cylinders for this purpose. It is illegal to ship original cylinders with used refrigerants.

▷ Never use disposable refrigerant cylinders as compressed air tanks. Refrigerant cylinders are not properly coated on the inside, and moisture from compressed air will cause corrosion. This can weaken the cylinder and cause a violent rupture. There may

(continued next page)

to which the cylinder should be exposed. As the cylinder temperature decreases, the liquid will actually occupy *less* space within the cylinder, thus allowing more room for expansion (not filling!). The maximum recommended temperature is actually 125°F (52°C), slightly below the fill temperature.

Because cylinders are assumed to be liquid "filled" at 130°F (54°C), and because manufacturers recommend that refrigerant cylinders do not exceed 125°F (52°C), there is a little room left—in theory, at least—for further expansion of the liquid before hydrostatic conditions are reached. At what temperature does the cylinder actually become 100% liquid filled? That's something you never want to find out, because it would be an accident waiting to happen! *Remember—never exceed 125°F (52°C).*

Hydrostatic pressures

Explosions—or the bursting of cylinders from overpressure—are frequently caused by overfilling the cylinders with liquids at lower temperatures. Then when a cylinder warms up, the liquid expands and exerts tremendous *hydrostatic* pressure.

In order for hydrostatic conditions to occur in a refrigerant cylinder, the cylinder must become 100% filled with liquid, with no vapor space remaining. The danger occurs when the cylinder temperature is increased. If a 100% liquid-filled cylinder is placed on the roof of a building during the summer, for example, the heat will cause a rapid increase in pressure in a very short time. Preventing the liquid in a sealed container from expanding under these *hydrostatic* conditions is impossible.

In the case of R-22, hydrostatic conditions will result in a pressure rise of approximately 60 psi with each increase of 1°F—which means that a 10°F increase in temperature will create a pressure increase of 600 psi! To make matters worse, a 20°F temperature rise will increase the hydrostatic pressure to 1,200 psi—well above the burst pressure of most cylinders (see Figure 5 on page 82). Fortunately, pressure relief devices—provided they are operating properly and have not been tampered with—can in many cases prevent cylinders from bursting.

Overpressurization

Obviously, cylinder overpressurization can be caused by overfilling. However, it can also happen if a mixture of different refrigerants or gases is placed into the cylinder. In many cases, this happens by accident, without intent to mix the different refrigerants. Mixing different refrigerants is always to be

---

(continued from previous page)

be no evidence of cylinder weakening until it fails.

▷ Always store refrigerant cylinders in a dry area. Storage in damp areas may permit corrosion, which will weaken the cylinders over time. Also, do not store in direct sunlight where cylinder temperatures can exceed 125°F (52°C).

Here are some additional safety guidelines to follow when charging a system:

▷ Remove liquid from the cylinder when charging any blend. Once removed from the cylinder, it can be flashed to vapor for charging.

▷ Verify proper hookup of charging hoses. Do not charge to the discharge side of the compressor.

▷ Open valves slowly.

▷ Protect cylinders from moisture and rusting during storage.

▷ Verify that the refrigerant label matches any color code or labeling used on the equipment.

▷ Identify a cylinder by reading the label affixed to it. Do not depend on the color of the cylinder for identification.

▷ Do not force connections.

▷ Do not drop, dent, or mechanically abuse containers.

SOURCE: DUPONT

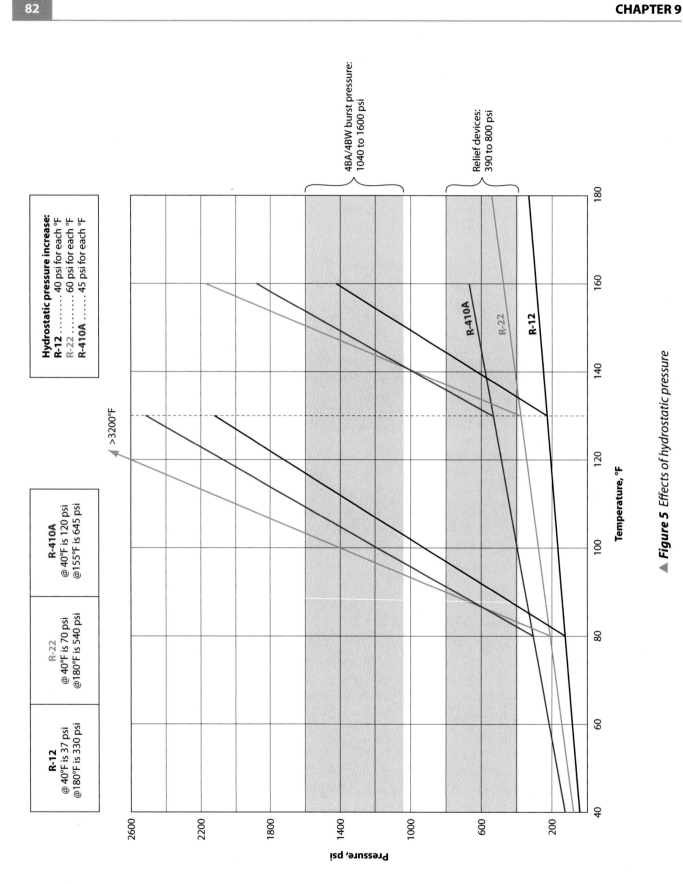

▲ **Figure 5** *Effects of hydrostatic pressure*

avoided, since the mixture will no longer be useful, and may be a candidate for proper disposal or destruction. Mixing of gases may occur when nitrogen or air and water vapor (noncondensable gases) removed from a system are added to a cylinder containing a refrigerant.

Based on Dalton's Law of Partial Pressures, the cylinder pressure will be determined by the sum of the partial pressures of all the gases present in the cylinder—that is, the pressures are *cumulative*. This means that small quantities of different gases in a cylinder could create unexpectedly high pressures. For example, compare the pressures of oxygen and "air" (which is basically a mixture of a variety of gases, such as oxygen, nitrogen, water vapor, and others) at the same temperature:

▶ Oxygen at –280°F (–173°C) has a pressure of 36.9 psia.
▶ Air at –280°F (–173°C) has a pressure of 88.0 psia.

Why is the pressure exerted by air so much more than the pressure exerted by oxygen? Because the pressure exerted by air is the result of the sum of the partial pressures of all the different gases that make up the air. Oxygen, on the other hand, has no other gases as part of its makeup—therefore, it exerts only the pressure developed by a single gas.

The same principle applies when an R-410A refrigerant cylinder has nitrogen, air, or another refrigerant added to it—and you get the same results. A higher-than-expected (saturation) pressure will be observed, which can lead to overpressurization of the cylinder and lower-than-permitted liquid fill amounts.

COMMON REFRIGERANT CYLINDER SAFETY PRECAUTIONS

Keep the following safety precautions in mind when working with refrigerant cylinders:
▶ Never store or expose cylinders to temperatures above 125°F (52°C).
▶ Never apply an open flame to a cylinder.
▶ Never use water or an electric blanket exceeding 110°F (43°C) to heat a cylinder.
▶ Open access valves slowly.
▶ Always use proper handles, wrenches, and fittings to access the refrigerant.
▶ Never refill single-trip (disposable) or manufacturer-refillable-only cylinders in the field.
▶ Never fill or refill a refillable cylinder with a substance that it was not designed to contain.

▶ Never exceed 80% liquid fill of a cylinder's WC (water capacity) at 60°F (15°C).

▶ Always store and transport cylinders in the upright position and in a secure manner.

▶ The relief valve must be in contact with the vapor space at all times for proper operation.

▶ Never use a cylinder that is past its retest date. (Cylinders typically have a 5-year retest date.)

▶ Use caution when recovering refrigerants that may be mixed or contaminated with noncondensable gases. Pressures will be higher than expected.

▶ Never expose cylinders to a corrosive environment. The integrity of the container may be compromised.

▶ Prevent cylinders from becoming damaged as a result of poor handling or transportation.

▶ Make sure that recovery cylinder pressures are rated for the correct refrigerant type—i.e., R-410A requires higher pressure-rated cylinders than R-22.

▶ Avoid overfilling recovery cylinders. If the cylinder is overfilled with liquid refrigerant and is stored in a high-temperature condition, hydrostatic pressures can cause the cylinder to rupture, leading to serious injury or even death. Make sure that the pressure relief valves on recovery cylinders are in place, tested periodically as required, and operating properly.

▶ Return cylinders to the proper source for refrigerant reclamation.

▶ Dispose of cylinders in the proper manner as required by various regulations/codes.

▶ Be aware of local codes that may not permit the use or transportation of disposable or nonrefillable cylinders.

▶ Ensure that cylinders are properly labeled and that the refrigerant is correctly identified.

▶ Never tamper with or restrict the operation of the safety relief device.

▶ If a weigh scale is used to measure the amount of refrigerant being added to a cylinder, ensure that the weigh scale is accurate and operates properly. Also take into account the liquid density of the refrigerant for various temperatures.

▶ Draw a vacuum on empty cylinders to ensure that they remain clean and dry inside. Doing so assists in reducing any internal corrosion.

SAFE HANDLING OF OTHER COMPRESSED GAS CYLINDERS

Many of the safety precautions that apply to handling refrigerant cylinders also apply to cylinders containing other gases. Make sure that you use *only* compressed gas cylinders that have been approved by the Department of Transportation (DOT) or Transport Canada (TC) for cutting, heating, and welding operations.

 WARNING: Serious accidents can result from the improper use and handling of compressed gas cylinders. *Always* follow the instructions and safety procedures provided by your supplier.

Observe the following general guidelines:
▶ Always keep cylinders in a vertical, upright position and secured from falling.
▶ Locate cylinders away from sparks, hot slag, and flames. Do not allow any electrical contact with the cylinders.
▶ Store empty cylinders with valves closed, protective caps in place, and separate from full cylinders.
▶ Keep cylinder valve protection caps on whenever cylinders are not being used.
▶ Use a suitable hand truck for transporting or moving cylinders.
▶ Never use compressed gas cylinders without an approved gas pressure-reducing regulator attached to the outlet of the cylinder.

Leaking cylinders, whether they contain acetylene, oxygen, hydrogen, nitrogen, or some other gas, should be isolated from other cylinders and stored in a well-ventilated area (preferably an outside protected location). Make sure that leaking cylinders are tagged as defective and returned to the supplier as soon as possible. *Never* use a leaking cylinder for *any* purpose. *Never* use a flame to check for leaks. It is much safer to use a soap solution instead.

Oxygen cylinders

Always use an approved pressure regulator and approved hoses for welding and brazing operations that utilize oxygen and fuel gases. When oxygen cylinders are not in use or when they are being transported, the regulators must be removed and the protective caps must be in place.

Carbon dioxide and nitrogen cylinders

When using carbon dioxide or nitrogen for pressure-testing or for blowing out coils, *always* use a proper pressure regulator on the cylinder. Make sure that the test rig is equipped with a 150-psi pressure relief valve. *Never* use a CO_2 or nitrogen cylinder to pressure-test a system without a regulator and relief valve.

Never transport a CO_2 or nitrogen cylinder with the regulator and pressure relief valve on the cylinder. Always remove the regulator and install the protective cap on the cylinder.

Ammonia cylinders

Like other cylinders, ammonia cylinders must be stored in an upright position and must be secured in place. When connecting, disconnecting, or otherwise working with ammonia cylinders, wear an approved face shield or safety goggles, protective gloves, and preferably cotton clothing. For work in refrigeration and mechanical rooms, it is also advisable to wear aprons, pants, and slickers made of rubber or other materials impervious to ammonia.

Make sure that connections, regulators, gauges, hoses, and other components are specifically designed and stamped for use with anhydrous ammonia. If ammonia vapor leaks between the stem and packing nut on the opening, close the valve, then tighten the nut by turning it counterclockwise. Reopen the valve. If the leaking persists, call the supplier immediately.

Never use compressed ammonia vapor where the cylinder can be contaminated by feedback unless the cylinder is protected by suitable check valves. ∎

CHAPTER 10

Soldering, Brazing, and Welding

GENERAL SAFETY PRECAUTIONS

Soldering, brazing, welding, and cutting operations present some specific hazards. When you work with electric welding equipment or torches, you must take special precautions to prevent fires. Flammable materials near the work area need to be protected from heat and sparks by using shields or wetting the materials. Fire extinguishers should always be kept in close proximity while torches are being used. When the location or type of work prevents a good view of the entire area in which sparks may fall or flames come in contact with flammable materials, another person should be posted to provide a fire watch.

Personal safety is critical. It is important to remember that torches—and, especially, arc welders—give off ultraviolet radiation that can be damaging to the eyes and skin. Always wear proper protection. Burns, too, are a significant hazard when welding and working with torches. Be sure to wear gloves and protective clothing. Proper ventilation is also important when torches or welding equipment is being used. Fumes given off from the fluxes and filler materials can be hazardous. When oils and refrigerants are heated, they can break down and create hazardous fumes. Be sure that refrigerants are removed from the system and lines are purged with nitrogen before heat is applied.

For torches, make sure that hoses, tanks, regulators, valves, and torch heads are visually inspected for any signs of damage before work begins. Set and check the pressure regulator to ensure that it is holding the proper pressure. A leak detector should be used to check the connections of the hoses for leaks. A flash arrestor should be used to prevent flashback in the hoses. Cylinders must always be stored and used in the upright position.

For arc welding equipment, make sure that you visually inspect both the power cables and the welding cables for any sign of damage before using. Cables with damaged insulation should be replaced immediately.

OSHA soldering, brazing, welding, and cutting checklist

Refer to the following checklist for guidelines on soldering, brazing, welding, and cutting safety:

☐ Are only authorized and trained personnel permitted to use welding, cutting, and brazing equipment?

☐ Does each operator have a copy of the appropriate operating instructions and are they directed to follow them?

☐ Are compressed gas cylinders regularly examined for obvious signs of defects, deep rusting, or leakage?

☐ Is care used in handling and storing cylinders, safety valves, and relief valves to prevent damage?

☐ Are precautions taken to prevent the mixture of air or oxygen with flammable gases, except at a burner or in a standard torch?

☐ Are only approved apparatus (torches, regulators, pressure-reducing valves, acetylene generators, and manifolds) used?

☐ Are cylinders kept away from sources of heat?

☐ Are the cylinders kept away from elevators, stairs, and gangways?

☐ Is it prohibited to use cylinders as rollers or supports?

☐ Are empty cylinders appropriately marked and their valves closed?

☐ Are signs reading **DANGER—NO SMOKING, MATCHES, OR OPEN LIGHTS,** or the equivalent, posted?

☐ Are cylinders, cylinder valves, couplings, regulators, hoses, and apparatus kept free of oily or greasy substances?

☐ Is care taken not to drop or strike cylinders?

☐ Unless secured on special trucks, are regulators removed and valve protection caps put in place before moving cylinders?

☐ Do cylinders without fixed hand wheels have keys, handles, or non-adjustable wrenches on stem valves when in service?

☐ Are liquefied gases stored and shipped valve-end up with valve covers in place?

☐ Are provisions made never to crack a fuel gas cylinder valve near sources of ignition?

☐ Before a regulator is removed, is the valve closed and gas released from the regulator?

☐ Is red used to identify the acetylene (or other fuel gas) hose, green for oxygen hose, and black for inert gas and air hose?

☐ Are pressure-reducing regulators used only for the gases and pressures for which they are intended?

▶ **SAFETY TIP** ◀

Beware of hazards when brazing

There are two possible sources of hazard to brazing operators. One consists of chemical fumes, and the other the heat and rays of the torch flame. Take the following general precautions to guard against these hazards:

▷ **Fumes.** Ventilate confined areas, using fans, exhaust hoods, or respirators if necessary. Clean all base metals to remove any surface contaminants that may create fumes when the metals are heated. Use flux (when required) in sufficient quantity to prevent oxidation and fuming during the heating cycle. Heat broadly and heat only the base metals—not the filler metal. Remove any toxic coatings and be careful not to overheat assemblies.

▷ **Torch heat and rays.** Wear gloves to protect hands against heat. Use shaded goggles or fixed glass shields to protect against eye fatigue and vision damage.

SOURCE: LUCASMILHAUPT BRAZING TIPS AND TECHNIQUES

☐ Is the open-circuit (no-load) voltage of arc welding and cutting machines as low as possible and not in excess of the recommended limits?

☐ Under wet conditions, are automatic controls for reducing no-load voltage used?

☐ Are the grounding of the machine frame and the safety ground connections of portable machines checked periodically?

☐ Are electrodes removed from the holders when not in use?

☐ Is it required that electric power to the welder be shut off when no one is in attendance?

☐ Is suitable fire-extinguishing equipment available for immediate use?

☐ Is the welder forbidden to coil or loop welding electrode cable around his or her body?

☐ Are wet machines thoroughly dried and tested before being used?

☐ Are work and electrode lead cables frequently inspected for wear and damage, and replaced when needed?

☐ Do means for connecting cable lengths have adequate insulation?

☐ When the object to be welded cannot be moved and fire hazards cannot be removed, are shields used to confine heat, sparks, and slag?

☐ Are fire watchers assigned when welding or cutting is performed in locations where a serious fire might develop?

☐ Are combustible floors kept wet, covered by damp sand, or protected by fire-resistant shields?

☐ When floors are wet down, are personnel protected from possible electric shock?

☐ When welding is done on metal walls, are precautions taken to protect combustibles on the other side?

☐ Before hot work is begun, are used drums, barrels, tanks, and other containers so thoroughly cleaned that no substances remain that could explode, ignite, or produce toxic vapors?

☐ Are employees exposed to the hazards created by welding, cutting, or brazing operations protected with personal protective equipment and clothing?

☐ Is it required that all PPE meet appropriate standards?

☐ Is a check made for adequate ventilation in and where welding or cutting is performed?

☐ When working in confined places, are environmental monitoring tests taken and means provided for quick removal of welders in case of an emergency?

PIPING AND CONNECTIONS

Sometimes it is necessary to cut refrigerant lines in order to repair leaks or replace components in refrigeration and air conditioning systems. The following precautions and procedures apply to breaking, cleaning, and rejoining piping and connections:

▶ *Never* apply heat to a line under refrigerant pressure. *Never* apply a flame to any part of a system containing refrigerant. Rupture can result.

▶ When a fluorocarbon refrigerant is heated, it breaks down to form corrosive acids and carcinogenic compounds. Hydrochloric and hydrofluoric acids can damage mucous membranes and lungs if they are inhaled, and blister skin if contacted. They also can cause rapid corrosion of metal. Carcinogenic products can cause cancer.

▶ To separate a soldered joint, first clean the outside and apply flux. Then heat the fitting evenly until the solder melts and the joint can be separated.

▶ Fittings and connections are always subject to some corrosion from the decomposition of refrigerant. Clean mating parts thoroughly before rejoining them.

▶ When soldering, brazing, or welding, provide proper ventilation to remove fumes created by the heating of refrigerant residues.

 WARNING: When isolating a component or a single section of piping for inspection or repair (see Figure 1), exercise caution to prevent damage and other potential hazards from liquid expansion. An increase in ambient temperature around a section of piping or a mechanical component that contains trapped liquid refrigerant and oil will create extremely high pressure within the isolated area. Such high pressures may result in a ruptured gasket, valve, pipe, or component—and for that reason they represent a very real threat to safety and health. Whenever possible during inspection and repair, avoid leaving refrigerant and/or oil trapped between valves or in lines and components.

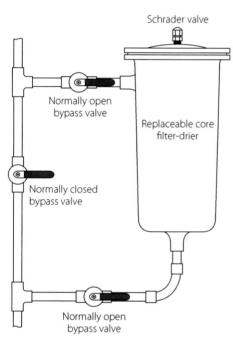

Schrader valve

Normally open bypass valve

Replaceable core filter-drier

Normally closed bypass valve

Normally open bypass valve

▲ *Figure 1* *Tee connections and valves allow this section of system to be drained*

FUMES AND FIRE HAZARDS

Fumes from welding and other hot work operations contain particles of the metals being welded together as well as those materials being used to do the welding or soldering. These may include cadmium, zinc, lead, iron, copper, the filler material, flux, and the coating on welding rods. Such operations also may generate other gases, like carbon monoxide, arsine, ozone, etc., at concentrations that may be hazardous to workers in the area. Ventilation, respiratory protection, safety glasses, or protective curtains may be necessary to reduce the hazards created by these conditions.

Areas where welding, cutting, or brazing are to be performed should be inspected for potential fire hazards. Ideally, there should be no combustible materials present. If combustibles in the immediate area are unavoidable, guards or shields should be used to protect the hazardous materials from heat and sparks. Suitable fire extinguishing equipment such as pails of water, buckets of sand, hoses, or portable fire extinguishers should be available for instant use.

Persons operating torches for cutting, welding, or brazing must be properly trained in the operation of their equipment. Always use proper protective equipment such as goggles, helmets, gloves, and leggings or high boots when performing hot work operations.

The potential health hazard to a welder or cutter from gases or fumes depends on the toxicity of the materials being worked with and the duration of the exposure. There should always be adequate ventilation, especially if the welder is working with stainless steel, lead, zinc, or cadmium. Some metals are coated with paint that contains lead or mercury. Fluxes and other materials also may contain fluorides. No welding, cutting, or other hot work should be performed on used drums, barrels, tanks, or other containers until they have been thoroughly cleaned. There should be no substances such as grease, tars, acids, or other materials which, when subjected to heat, might produce flammable or toxic vapors.

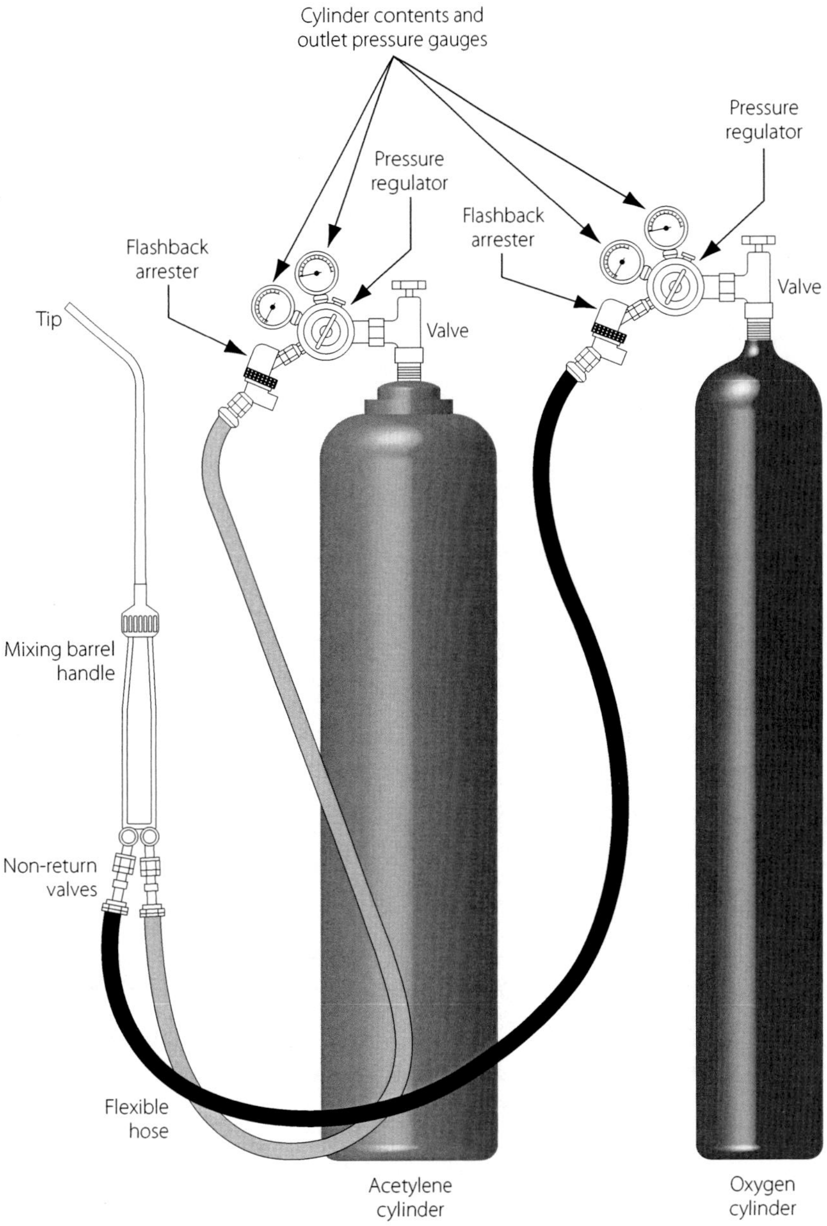

▲ Figure 2 *Oxyacetylene welding equipment*

WORKING WITH OXYGEN AND ACETYLENE

Figure 2 shows a typical oxyacetylene welding setup. There are two very important hazards to remember when working with oxygen and acetylene:

▶ Do not allow oxygen and oil to come in contact with one another. They will react with each other and cause a violent spontaneous explosion.

▶ Do not use acetylene at a pressure higher than 15 psig (30 psia). Above this pressure, acetylene may become unstable.

▶ All oxygen and acetylene equipment should be equipped with both flashback arresters and non-return valves/check valves.

All cylinders should be clearly marked as to their contents. When they are stored, they should have protective caps installed over the valves and be fastened and secured to prevent them from toppling over. They should be stored away from any source of heat. Oxygen cylinders should be stored separately from fuel gas cylinders.

Observe the following precautions when handling oxygen and acetylene cylinders:

▶ Oxygen and acetylene cylinders must be secured in an upright position at all times during storage, use, and transportation (see Figure 3).

▶ Store cylinders in a well-ventilated area (preferably outdoors, with overhead protection from the weather).

▶ Keep acetylene cylinders away from heat sources. The surrounding temperature should be kept below 130°F (54°C).

▶ Store full and empty cylinders separately. Store acetylene and oxygen cylinders separately.

▶ Protective caps must be in place when the cylinders are not in use or when they are being moved.

▶ Place cylinders where materials and equipment will not strike them, fall on them, or knock them over.

▶ Do not store or use cylinders where they can become part of an electric circuit or be struck by a welding rod.

▶ Before moving cylinders, close the valves, remove the regulators, and replace the protective caps.

▶ Cylinders must be hoisted in properly rigged racks or baskets to keep them secure and upright.

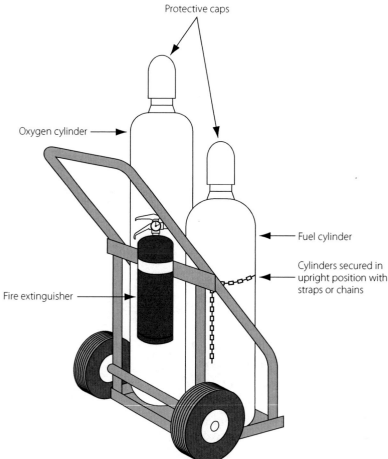

▲ *Figure 3* *Typical welding cart*

▶ Before using regulators, hoses, or torches, make sure that they work properly. Protect supply hoses from traffic.

▶ At least one 4A40BC fire extinguisher must be available wherever oxyacetylene cutting, welding, soldering, or brazing operations are performed.

▶ When using an oxyacetylene cutting torch, workers must wear leather gauntlet gloves and goggles with a No. 4 or 5 lens shade. (Be aware that No. 4 or 5 lenses do *not* remove arc welding rays. For arc welding, No. 10 or 12 lenses are required.)

▶ Workers performing oxyacetylene work should not carry butane lighters.

▶ Do not use oxyacetylene torches to blow dust from work surfaces, clothing, or skin.

▶ Use the proper T-wrench or key to open acetylene cylinders and leave the wrench or key on the valve for emergency shutoff.

▶ Use only a spark lighter to ignite torches. *Never* use matches or cigarette lighters.

▶ A leaking gas cylinder must be shut off and removed to an outdoor location away from ignition sources. Mark the cylinder so that it is readily identifiable, and notify the supplier immediately.

▶ When handling a leaking cylinder, remember that your clothing can be saturated with gas and you can draw a trail of gas behind you. Stay away from all ignition sources.

▶ *Never* use oxygen or acetylene to pressure-test for leaks in a refrigeration or air conditioning system. These gases can react explosively with oil in the system.

WORKING WITH PROPANE

Figure 4 shows a typical propane cylinder. Observe the following precautions when handling propane cylinders:

▶ Unless designed for horizontal use, propane cylinders must be kept in an upright position.

▶ Store propane cylinders in a well-ventilated area away from heat sources (preferably outdoors and above grade).

▶ When not in use, propane cylinders and hose-connected devices should *not* be left in trenches or other low-lying areas. Propane is heavier than air and can settle in dangerous concentrations at the bottom of vaults, vessels, equipment wells, basements, and similar locations.

▶ Use only approved hoses, fittings, and correct wrenches to connect a cylinder to tools and equipment.

▶ *Never* check for leaks in a propane cylinder with a match or torch. Use soapy water for this task (see Figure 5 on the next page).

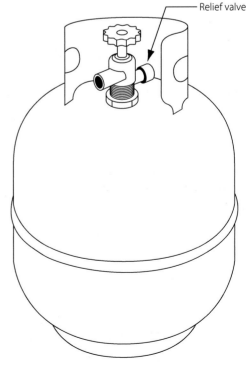

Relief valve

▲ *Figure 4* Typical propane cylinder

▶ When handling a leaking cylinder, remember that your clothing can be saturated with propane and you can draw a trail of gas behind you. Stay away from all ignition sources.

▶ Wherever possible, position safety relief valves so that they face *away* from likely sources of heat.

TORCH SAFETY

The remainder of this Chapter contains important safety and operational information for oxy-fuel cutting, welding, and heating equipment. Do not use such equipment unless you have received training in the proper procedures from a qualified instructor.

When working with or around oxy-fuel equipment, note especially the specific meaning of the words "Danger," "Warning," and "Caution" as they are used on labels and in operating instructions:

▶ **DANGER** is used to indicate the presence of a hazard that *will* cause *severe* personal injury, death, or substantial property damage if ignored.

▶ **WARNING** is used to indicate the presence of a hazard that *can* cause *severe* personal injury, death, or substantial property damage if ignored.

▶ **CAUTION** is used to indicate the presence of a hazard that *can* cause *minor* personal injury or property damage if ignored.

Figure 6 shows a typical torch used for cutting, welding, brazing, and heating.

Personal protective equipment

Oxy-fuel cutting, welding, and heating produce hazardous rays of light (infrared/ultraviolet). Eye protection is required for operating oxy-fuel equipment. Wear safety glasses in conjunction with an approved filter lens (shade 5 or darker).

Molten metal or sparks produced by oxy-fuel operations can cause severe burns to unprotected parts of the body. Always wear appropriate protective clothing such as gloves, aprons, safety shoes, etc.

 WARNING: Keep all clothing and protective equipment free of oil and grease. These substances can ignite and burn violently in the presence of pure oxygen.

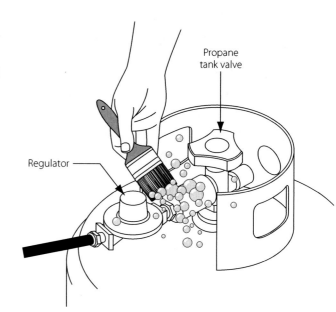

Propane tank valve

Regulator

▲ *Figure 5* Soap test for leaks

Work area

Whenever possible, oxy-fuel cutting, welding, and heating operations should be performed in an open, well-ventilated area. Always ensure that the work area has been properly ventilated and that adequate ventilation is maintained while oxy-fuel equipment is in use. Atmospheres in confined spaces must be tested for explosives and toxic gases prior to the use of oxy-fuel equipment. Respiratory protection must be used when cutting or welding with certain combinations of metals, coatings, and gases (refer to ANSI Standard Z49-1).

The safety of any work area can be improved by following good housekeeping practices:

▶ The work place must have a fireproof floor (such as concrete).

▶ Work benches used for cutting and welding operations must have fireproof tops. A common material used is firebrick.

▶ Nearby walls and unprotected flooring should be protected from sparks and hot metal by the use of heat-resistant shields or other approved material.

▶ An approved fire extinguisher must be kept and properly maintained (checked regularly) in the work area.

▶ The work site should be cleared of combustible materials. If the combustible materials cannot be removed, they must be protected with fireproof covers and a fire watch should be established.

▶ Oxygen must *never* be allowed to come in contact with grease, oil, or other petroleum-based substances. In the presence of oxygen, such substances become highly explosive and can ignite and burn violently.

 WARNING: *Never* perform welding operations in an area containing combustible vapors, flammable liquids, or explosive dust. Tanks or other closed containers that have held such materials should not be cut or welded.

OXY-FUEL EQUIPMENT

Read, follow, and be sure you understand the following instructions before installing or operating any oxy-fuel equipment:

▶ Do not use regulators, hoses, cylinders, torches, or any oxy-fuel equipment if oil, grease, or similar contaminants are present.

▶ Do not use regulators, hoses, cylinders, torches, or any oxy-fuel equipment if it has been damaged.

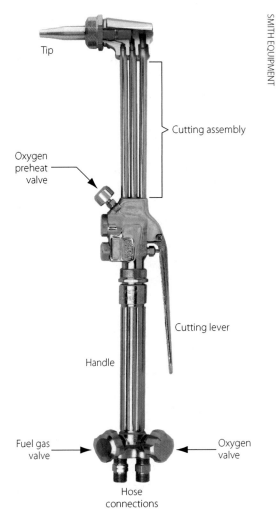

SMITH EQUIPMENT

Tip

Cutting assembly

Oxygen preheat valve

Cutting lever

Handle

Fuel gas valve

Oxygen valve

Hose connections

▲ *Figure 6* Typical oxy-fuel torch

▶ Do not alter or attempt to repair any oxy-fuel equipment. Repairs should be performed only by a competent repair center.

Compressed gas cylinders

Use only compressed gas cylinders that have been approved by the Department of Transportation (DOT) for cutting, welding, brazing, and heating operations.

▶ Make sure that cylinders are always kept in a vertical position and secured from falling.

▶ Keep cylinder valve protection caps on when cylinders are not being used.

▶ A suitable hand truck must be used for transporting or moving cylinders.

▶ Locate cylinders away from sparks, hot slag, and flames. Do not allow any electrical contact with the cylinders.

▶ Empty cylinders should be stored with the valves closed, protective caps in place, and separated from full cylinders.

▶ Never use compressed gas cylinders without an approved gas pressure-reducing regulator attached to the outlet of the cylinder.

▶ Never tamper with or attempt to repair compressed gas cylinders or valves. Leaking cylinders or cylinders with leaking valves should be placed outdoors, identified, and returned to the supplier.

 WARNING: Serious accidents can result from the improper use and handling of compressed gas cylinders. *Always follow the instructions and safety procedures provided by your supplier.*

Reverse-flow check valves

It is recommended that reverse-flow check valves be installed in the system either on the regulator or the torch body, reducing the possibility of gases mixing in the hoses and/or the regulators. In the event of a flashback fire, the combustible gases will burn rapidly. This can result in an explosion in the hoses, the regulators, or the cylinders.

Reverse-flow check valves should be tested every three months at a minimum—check them more often if the hoses are frequently disconnected from the regulators.

Test method for reverse-flow check valves

1. With the regulator removed from the cylinder or manifold, remove the hose from the check valve.
2. Turn the regulator adjusting screw (clockwise) until greater resistance is felt. This will open the regulator.

3. Place the regulator inlet nipple in a vessel of water.
4. Blow into the outlet side of the check valve.
5. If bubbles escape from the inlet side of the regulator, it indicates a faulty check valve. (Do not use the equipment until the faulty check valve has been replaced).
6. Remove and replace the faulty check valve with a new one, and reattach the hoses.
7. If no bubbles were present in Step 5, reattach the hoses to the check valve and regulator.

EQUIPMENT SETUP

Attaching regulators

Regulators must be used *only* with the gases and at the pressures for which they are designed. Note that the recommended operating temperature range for pressure regulators is 0 to 140°F (–18 to +60°C). Follow these steps when attaching regulators:

1. Make sure that the cylinders are fastened securely to prevent them from tipping or falling.
2. Remove the oxygen cylinder valve protective cap from the cylinder.
3. Slightly crack open the oxygen cylinder valve, allowing gas to escape, then close it again quickly. This will clean the connection of any foreign matter.
4. Attach the oxygen regulator to the oxygen cylinder and secure it tightly. Always tighten regulator connection nuts with a wrench.
5. Follow the same procedure for the fuel gas cylinder as described above in Steps 1 through 3.
6. Attach the fuel gas regulator to the fuel gas cylinder and secure it tightly, again using a wrench.

 WARNING: When opening the oxygen and fuel gas cylinders to clean the valves, be sure that the area is well-ventilated. Direct the oxygen and fuel gas away from people and from open flames or other sources of ignition. Fire and explosion can result from the rapidly escaping gases.

Installing hoses

Use only industrial-grade hoses for cutting, welding, brazing, and heating equipment. These hoses transport low-pressure gases from the regulators to the torch. Industrial welding hoses are generally color-coded green for oxygen (with a right-hand threaded connection) and red for fuel gas (with a left-hand threaded connection and a groove around the nut). Do not attempt to splice or use damaged hoses.

▶ **SAFETY TIP** ◀

Follow precautions for welding, cutting

Because oxyacetylene welding and flamecutting are frequently required when installing and repairing refrigeration and air conditioning equipment, the following precautions are important:

▷ Don't use oxygen as a substitute for compressed air or for any purpose other than welding or flamecutting.

▷ Don't store oxygen cylinders near combustible material, especially oil and grease. Don't handle oxygen cylinders or apparatus with oily hands or gloves. Oxygen supports and accelerates combustion and will cause oil, grease, and plastic materials to burn with great intensity.

▷ Don't weld or flamecut near combustible materials or in an atmosphere containing refrigerant. Wait until pressure vessels and piping have been completely evacuated.

▷ Don't weld or flamecut in a confined area unless the area is adequately ventilated.

▷ Don't carry a plastic liquid-fuel cigarette lighter or other flammable materials while welding, soldering, or brazing. Welding sparks, molten metal, and heat from a torch can ignite the contents of the lighter and cause it to explode.

SOURCE: CARRIER SAFETY GUIDE FOR REFRIGERATION AND AIR-CONDITIONING EQUIPMENT

When new hoses are being installed for the first time, the hoses must be cleaned of the preservative talc:

1. Attach the green hose to the oxygen regulator and tighten securely with a wrench.
2. Attach the red hose to the fuel gas regulator and tighten securely with a wrench.
3. Turn the oxygen regulator adjusting screw to the left (counterclockwise) until there is no resistance on the adjusting screw (see Figure 7).
4. While standing to the side of the regulator, slowly open the oxygen cylinder valve. Never open a cylinder valve suddenly—doing so can damage a regulator or even cause an oxygen regulator fire.

 WARNING: Do not stand in front of or behind the regulator when opening the cylinder valve. Always place the cylinder between you and the regulator.

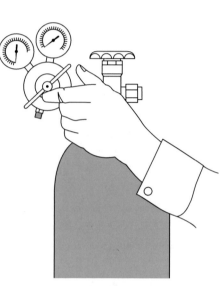

▲ **Figure 7** *Release regulator adjusting screw fully before opening cylinder valve*

5. Continue to open the oxygen cylinder valve slowly until the maximum cylinder pressure is indicated on the high-pressure regulator gauge (the gauge nearest the cylinder valve). Then open the oxygen cylinder valve all the way.
6. Turn the oxygen regulator adjusting screw clockwise until the low-pressure gauge indicates 3 to 5 psig. Allow the oxygen to flow for approximately 5 to 10 seconds to clean the hose of dust, dirt, or preservatives that may be present. Perform this process in a well-ventilated area. Direct the hose away from people and from open flames or other sources of ignition.
7. After cleaning the hose, shut off the oxygen flow by turning the adjusting screw to the left (counterclockwise) until there is an absence of spring pressure and the low-pressure gauge reads 0 psig.
8. Close the oxygen cylinder valve.
9. Repeat the same procedure to clean the fuel gas hose.
10. Attach the oxygen hose to the oxygen connection on the torch handle. Tighten securely with a wrench.
11. Attach the fuel gas hose to the fuel gas connection on the torch handle. Tighten securely with a wrench.

Selecting and installing a welding tip

Using the torch manufacturer's guide, select the welding tip to be used. Then:

1. Insert the tip into the torch body.

2. Exert light pressure on the welding tip with a twisting motion until it seats into the torch body.
3. Position the tip and hand tighten the tip nut into the torch handle.

Adjusting the pressure at the regulators

1. Check to make sure that both regulator adjusting screws are turned out (to the "OFF" position). If the adjusting screw is turned in, high-pressure gas may damage the internal parts of the regulator, resulting in an explosion or fire.
2. Using the manufacturer's tip charts, determine the oxygen and fuel gas pressures to use with the selected welding tip.
3. Close the fuel gas torch valve.
4. Close the oxygen torch valve.
5. Slowly open the oxygen cylinder valve and adjust the regulator by turning in the adjusting screw to deliver the recommended pressure.
6. Slowly open the fuel gas cylinder valve and adjust the regulator by turning in the adjusting screw to deliver the recommended pressure.

Purging the system

 WARNING: Before lighting the torch, always purge the system to reduce the possibility of a mixed-gas condition in the equipment. Mixed gases in the equipment can result in a fire or violent explosion. Purging must be done in a well-ventilated area away from any open flames or other sources of ignition.

1. Open the oxygen torch valve ¼ turn, and allow oxygen to pass through the torch for 3 to 5 seconds for every 25 ft (7.6 m) of hose. With the oxygen flowing, reset the recommended working pressure on the oxygen regulator, if necessary.
2. Close the oxygen torch valve.
3. Open the fuel gas torch valve ¼ turn and allow fuel gas to pass through the torch for 3 to 5 seconds for every 25 ft (7.6 m) of hose. With the fuel gas flowing, reset the recommended working pressure on the fuel gas regulator, if necessary.
4. Close the fuel gas torch valve.

The system is now purged and ready for operation. *Purge the system every time before igniting the torch.*

Testing the equipment for leaks

Check the equipment for leaks using an approved oil-free leak detection fluid. With the system and the torch body valves closed, test for leaks at all connections on the regulators, cylinders, and torch body. If any leaks are detected, do not use the equipment until the leaks are corrected.

ASSOCIATED HAZARDS OF RECOMPRESSING PURE OXYGEN

Recompressing high-pressure oxygen in a low-pressure cavity may create conditions that result in combustion. There are three ingredients necessary for combustion to occur—fuel, heat, and oxygen. All three of these ingredients may be present when oxygen is recompressed into a regulator quickly:

▶ **Fuel.** The fuel for combustion may be in the regulator itself if enough heat is produced to reach the kindling temperature of the regulator components.

▶ **Heat.** Enough heat may be generated by the friction created when recompressing high-pressure oxygen to ignite the regulator components. This heat is known as the *heat of recompression*.

▶ **Oxygen.** The oxygen is provided by the cylinder in a very pure form. Pure oxygen affects combustion differently than does atmospheric air. High-purity oxygen accelerates the rate of combustion, increases the heat output, and lowers the combustible point of any material.

Preventive measures

Before attaching the oxygen regulator to the cylinder, clear any debris from the cylinder outlet port by slightly cracking open the oxygen cylinder valve, allowing gas to escape, and then closing it again quickly. Always make sure that the regulator adjusting screw is in the full out ("OFF") position before opening the oxygen cylinder valve. When opening an oxygen cylinder, crack the cylinder valve slowly.

 WARNING: In the event of an internal fire or flashback (identified by a whistling sound or an inverted flame), turn off the oxygen torch valve immediately, then turn off the fuel gas torch valve. Next, turn off the oxygen cylinder valve. Finally, turn off the fuel gas cylinder valve. Do not relight the torch until the equipment has cooled to the touch and the cause of the flashback situation has been identified and corrected.

USING ACETYLENE AS THE FUEL GAS FOR WELDING OR BRAZING

Oxyacetylene equipment is designed to operate at a set volume of gas for each tip. Using less than the required volume may result in overheating the tip or the equipment and can lead to an internal fire or flashback. Always match the tip size to the metal that is to be cut or welded. Follow the manufacturer's recommendations for proper tip selection.

CAUTION: Before lighting the torch, follow all personal and equipment safety regulations. Use safety eye wear to protect your eyes from heat, sparks, and hazardous rays of light produced by the flame. Keep the torch pointed away from people and combustibles.

Having followed the instructions contained in this Chapter pertaining to setup and purging, you are ready to light the torch:
1. Open the acetylene torch valve ⅛ turn and ignite the fuel gas using an approved friction spark lighter (see Figure 8). *Never* use matches or a cigarette lighter to ignite the gas.
2. Increase the acetylene gas flow until the flame is no longer producing (soot) smoke.
3. Slowly open the oxygen torch valve until you achieve a neutral flame (an even mixture of fuel and oxygen).

USING A FUEL GAS OTHER THAN ACETYLENE

Alternative fuel gas tips require a slightly different procedure from acetylene tips to ensure proper performance. Having followed the instructions contained in this Chapter pertaining to setup and purging, you are now ready to light the torch:
1. Open the fuel gas torch valve ⅛ turn and ignite the fuel gas using an approved friction spark lighter.
2. Slowly open the oxygen torch valve until the flame is neutralized.
3. Increase the fuel gas torch valve another ⅛ turn.
4. Increase the oxygen flow until the flame is neutralized.
5. Repeat this procedure until the maximum volume of fuel is used and the desired flame is achieved. This is important to obtain the most efficient flame and to cool the tip during operation. *Failure to force a sufficient amount of fuel gas through the tip will cause the tip to overheat and may cause a flashback or backfire.*

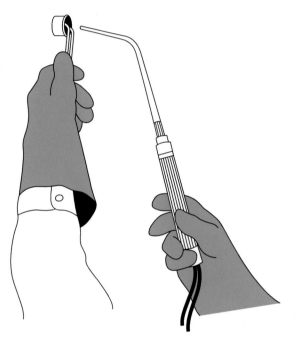
▲ *Figure 8* Ignite torch with friction spark lighter

 WARNING: When opening the torch valve to clear the system, make sure that the area is well-ventilated. Direct the gases away from people and from flames or other source of ignition. Fire and explosion can result from the escaping gases.

SYSTEM SHUTDOWN
Extinguishing the torch flame

1. Turn the oxygen torch valve (clockwise) to the closed position.
2. Turn the fuel gas torch valve (clockwise) to the closed position.

Bleeding the system

1. Turn the oxygen and fuel gas cylinder valves (clockwise) to the closed position.
2. Open the oxygen torch valve ½ turn and allow the gas to flow out of the torch until both gauges indicate 0 psig. Close the oxygen torch valve and back out the regulator adjusting screw to the "OFF" position.
3. Open the fuel gas torch valve ½ turn and allow the gas to flow out of the torch until both gauges indicate 0 psig. Close the fuel gas torch valve and back out the regulator adjusting screw to the "OFF" position.

Note: The sections of this Chapter that deal with oxy-fuel equipment safety (pages 94–102), as well as the two tables on the pages that follow, were adapted from material provided by Smith Equipment and reprinted with permission. ▪

▼ *Table 1* Welding/brazing tips for acetylene

| Metal thickness, in. | Welding tip series | | | Drill size | Acetylene and oxygen | |
	AW200	MW200	SW200		Pressure, psig (each gas at regulator)	Consumption, scfh (each gas)
Very light metal up to $1/32$				78	10	0.65
	AW200			76	10	1.3
				74	10	1.7
	AW201	MW201	SW201	71	10	2.3
$1/16$ to $3/32$				69	10	3.0
	AW203	MW203	SW203	67	10	3.2
	AW204	MW204	SW204	63	10	4.3
$1/8$	AW205	MW205	SW205	57	10	6
$5/32$				56	10	9
$3/16$	AW207	MW207	SW207	54	10	12
$1/4$		MW208		52	10	17
$3/8$	AW209	MW209	SW209	49	10	23
$1/2$	AW210	MW210	SW210	44	15	36
$5/8$				40	15	49
$7/8$			SW212	34	15	66
1 and over			SW213	30	15	90
			SW214	26	15	121

Consumption (scfh = standard cubic feet per hour) figures shown represent the average volumes of gases consumed when the sooty smoke disappears from the acetylene flame prior to opening the oxygen valve and adjusting to a neutral flame.

SOURCE: SMITH EQUIPMENT

▼ **Table 2** Quickbraze™ tip technical data

Stock No.	Gas pressure settings, psig		Consumption rate, cfh		Output, Btuh
	Oxygen	Fuel	Oxygen	Fuel	
S4	8	8	0.8	0.6	1,120
S6	8	8	3.2	3.4	7,360
S8	8	8	7.5	8.3	14,900
T5	8	8	3.9	3.9	7,240
T7	8	8	9.8	7.6	12,200
C2	7	5	6.4	7.2	12,350
C6	10	8	9.6	10.8	19,720
14711	12	10	14.7	9.7	13,760
A3	8	8	8	7	9,930
LP2	25	10	26	6	14,500
LP4	30	12	33	10	23,210

SOURCE: SMITH EQUIPMENT

Fire Safety

KIDDE

▲ *Figure 1* Typical multipurpose fire extinguisher

INTRODUCTION

Knowing how to control a fire can be just as important to a service technician as knowing how to diagnose and solve a difficult service problem. Safety-minded service technicians must be constantly alert to a variety of occupational hazards, but few are more potentially dangerous than the use of highly flammable gases in soldering, brazing, welding, and cutting operations (often in close proximity to other flammable materials). A service technician's knowledge of fires and how to extinguish them can spell the difference between enjoying the satisfaction of a job well done and being held responsible for loss of life and destruction of property.

The portable fire extinguisher (see Figure 1) is one of the most common fire protection appliances in use today. In many cases, a portable extinguisher can be used to put out a fire in much less time than other methods. Portable extinguishers should meet the criteria established by the National Fire Protection Association (NFPA) in the publication *NFPA 10: Standard for Portable Fire Extinguishers*. They also should have a satisfactory rating from Underwriters Laboratories (UL) or Underwriters' Laboratories of Canada (ULC).

Service technicians must be acquainted with various types of fire extinguishers—and with the various types of fires for which they are designed. A technician armed with this knowledge will be better equipped to deal with an emergency if and when it happens. Simply stated, fire is a chemical reaction. Three conditions are necessary in order to produce fire—some sort of *fuel*, enough *heat* to raise its temperature to the point of ignition, and enough *oxygen* to sustain combustion. These three ingredients—fuel, heat, and oxygen—are often referred to as the "fire triangle" (see Figure 2). When a combustible product (*fuel*) reaches its flash point (*heat*) in the presence of air (*oxygen*), an exothermic (heat-releasing) chemical reaction takes place and the combustible material will start to burn. But remove any one of these three components and the fire will go out.

Take, for example, the simple act of shutting off a gas burner on a stove. Turn a knob that closes a gas valve, and you have eliminated the *fuel*. Firefighters employ the same principle when they create a firebreak in the path of a forest fire. When you put out a campfire by pouring water on it, the water lowers the temperature of the fuel—in this case, you are removing *heat*. Throw a shovelful of dirt on the fire or smother it with a fire blanket, and you will "suffocate" it—because you are taking away the *oxygen* that a fire needs in order to "breathe."

▲ *Figure 2*
Fire triangle: fuel + heat + oxygen = fire

CLASSIFICATION OF FIRES

Fire extinguishers are portable devices used to put out fires of limited size. Such fires are grouped into four classes, according to the type of material that is burning:

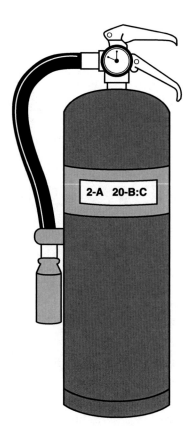

LETTERS (representing the four classes of fire) are used to indicate the type of fuel on which the extinguisher will be effective. The extinguisher at left is a multipurpose unit suitable for use with Class A, B, and C fires.

  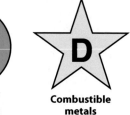

Ordinary combustibles   **Flammable liquids**   **Electrical equipment**   **Combustible metals**

NUMBERS are used along with the letters on Class A and B extinguishers. The numbers indicate the relative effectiveness of the extinguisher. To use the rating of the extinguisher at left as an example:

An extinguisher rated 2-A will extinguish twice as much fuel as a 1-A extinguisher.
An extinguisher rated 20-B will extinguish 20 times as much fuel as a 1-B extinguisher.

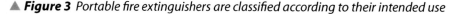

▲ *Figure 3* Portable fire extinguishers are classified according to their intended use

- ▶ *Class A* fires are those in which ordinary combustibles such as paper, wood, cloth, and trash are burning.
- ▶ *Class B* fires are those in which flammable liquids —oils, greases, gasoline, paint, or similar materials—are burning.
- ▶ *Class C* fires are those involving live (energized) electrical equipment.
- ▶ *Class D* fires are those in which combustible metals such as magnesium, potassium, and sodium are burning.

Each class of fire requires its own type of fire extinguisher. Some extinguishers can be used for only one class of fire. Others can be used for two or even three classes. None is suitable for all four classes. Each extinguisher is labeled according to the type(s) of fire it is designed to combat. As a further means of identification, the letters are displayed within different shapes—"A" in a triangle, "B" in a square, "C" in a circle, and "D" in a star (see Figure 3).

Numbers also are used on Class A and B extinguishers to indicate the relative size of the fire on which the extinguisher will be effective. The higher the rating, the greater its extinguishing capacity. For example, an extinguisher classified "4-A" can be expected to extinguish a Class A fire twice as large as that of a unit classified "2-A." In addition to the A, B, C designation, most fire extinguishers today have a symbol or "pictograph" label showing which fuels the extinguisher is designed to fight (see Figure 4).

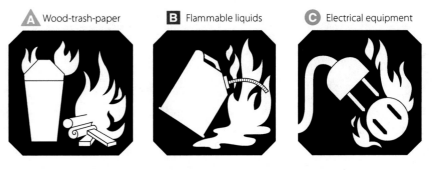

A Wood-trash-paper B Flammable liquids C Electrical equipment

▲ *Figure 4* Most extinguishers carry labels that use simple picture symbols to represent different types of fires

Fire extinguishers may go unused for many years, but they must be maintained in a state of readiness. For this reason, periodic inspection and servicing are required, and that responsibility rests with the owner. Fire department inspectors check at periodic intervals to see that extinguishers are present where required by law, and that they have been serviced within the specified time period. Check the inspection frequency dictated by your locality, insurance provider, and extinguisher manufacturer. As a general rule, portable fire extinguishers should be thoroughly inspected *at least* once a year. Your local government, insurance provider, or employer may have more stringent requirements.

Standards for the selection, placement, and testing of portable fire extinguishers are issued by the NFPA. The standards establish the minimum requirements for all types and sizes of extinguishers that are listed and rated by testing laboratories.

TYPES OF PORTABLE FIRE EXTINGUISHERS

Lists of approved fire extinguishers that may be purchased from different manufacturers are available from Underwriters Laboratories, Inc. (UL). An approved extinguisher has a label on it that provides operating instructions and identifies the class, or classes, of fires on which the extinguisher may be used safely. Approved extinguishers also carry the labels of the laboratories at which they were tested. Table 1 on pages 110 and 111 gives a brief overview of the many different types of portable fire extinguishers, and summarizes much of the information contained in the paragraphs below. It is very important that you use the proper extinguisher when fighting a fire. Not only might the flames *not* be extinguished if you use the wrong type of extinguisher, but the fire could actually increase.

Extinguishers for Class A fires

Fire extinguishers for Class A fires ("ordinary" combustibles) are usually water-based units. Water provides a heat-absorbing (cooling) effect on the burning material, and thus extinguishes fire by lowering the temperature of the fuel. Most Class A fire extinguishers are either *stored-pressure* extinguishers, which use air under pressure to expel the water, or *pump tank* extinguishers, which require the operator to push the plunger of a hand pump up and down to force the water out.

A pump tank extinguisher should be checked periodically to make sure that the water level is adequate and that the pump washers are in good condition, so that when and if it becomes necessary to use the pump, it will be capable of forcing the water out of the tank. When an extinguisher that contains water is subjected to freezing temperatures, the water should be treated with some type of anti-freeze solution.

Extinguishers for Class B fires

Class B fires (flammable liquids) are extinguished by displacing oxygen, by slowing down the release of flammable vapors, or by interrupting the chain reaction of the combustion. Three types of extinguishing agents—carbon dioxide, dry chemicals, and foam—are used for Class B fires.

Carbon dioxide (CO_2) is a gas that is heavier than air. CO_2 extinguishers work by displacing the oxygen in the air surrounding the flames, thus "starving" the fire and preventing further combustion. Because the release of the compressed gas reduces the oxygen content of the air, you may need protective breathing apparatus if you use a CO_2 extinguisher in a small space or confined area. Avoid contact with the discharged gas, which is very cold.

Dry chemical extinguishers work by interrupting the chemical reaction of combustion. Most use stored pressure to discharge the contents of the unit. There are two types of dry chemical extinguishers. One type contains sodium bicarbonate, potassium bicarbonate, or potassium chloride base agents. A second type, which uses ammonium phosphate as the active ingredient, is known as a *multipurpose* dry chemical extinguisher, because it can be used for Class A, B, and C fires.

Foam extinguishers use an *aqueous film-forming foam* (AFFF) agent that expels a layer of foam when it is discharged through a nozzle. It acts as a barrier to exclude oxygen from the fire. AFFF units can be used for Class A fires as well, but because they contain water must *not* be used for Class C fires.

Extinguishers for Class C fires

Obviously, extinguishers for Class C fires (electrical wiring, plugs, equipment, etc.) must utilize an extinguishing agent that does not conduct electricity. Both CO_2 extinguishers and dry chemical extinguishers can be effective in fighting electrical fires. An advantage of carbon dioxide is that it leaves no residue after the fire is extinguished. However, the qualities that make carbon dioxide safe for fighting electrical fires also make it dangerous to human life. Remember that when carbon dioxide replaces oxygen in the air to the extent that combustion cannot be sustained, respiration (breathing) also cannot be sustained. Exposure to an atmosphere where there are high concentrations of carbon dioxide can cause suffocation.

As stated previously, foam extinguishers should not be employed for Class C fires, although Class A and B extinguishers may be used if electrical equipment at the site of the fire is *not energized*. As long as electrical equipment or appliances are "plugged in," consider it a Class C fire.

Extinguishers for Class D fires

Dry powder extinguishers are used for Class D fires (combustible metals), because such fires require a heat-absorbing extinguishing agent that will not react with the burning metal. The dry powder covers the burning metal with a smothering layer that isolates the metal from oxygen. Avoid inhaling the dust when using a dry powder extinguisher to put out a fire. *Note:* Many

▼ **Table 1** *Characteristics of portable fire extinguishers*

Extinguishing agent	Method of operation	Capacity U.S.	Metric	UL or ULC classification
Water	Stored pressure	2½ gal	9.5 L	2-A
Water	Pump tank	1½ gal	5.7 L	1-A
	Pump tank	2½ gal	9.5 L	2-A
	Pump tank	4 gal	15.1 L	3-A
	Pump tank	5 gal	18.9 L	4-A
Water (antifreeze calcium chloride)	Cartridge or stored pressure	1¼, 1½ gal	4.73, 5.7 L	1-A
	Cartridge or stored pressure	2½ gal	9.5 L	2-A
	Cylinder	33 gal	125 L	20-A
Water (wetting agent)	Stored pressure	1½ gal	5.7 L	2-A
	Carbon dioxide cylinder	25 gal (wheeled)	94.6 L	10-A
	Carbon dioxide cylinder	45 gal (wheeled)	170.3 L	30-A
	Carbon dioxide cylinder	60 gal (wheeled)	227 L	40-A
Water (soda acid)	Chemically generated expellant	1¼, 1½ gal	4.73, 5.7 L	1-A
	Chemically generated expellant	2½ gal	9.5 L	2-A
	Chemically generated expellant	17 gal (wheeled)	64.3 L	10-A
	Chemically generated expellant	33 gal (wheeled)	125 L	20-A
Water (loaded stream)	Stored pressure	2½ gal	9.5 L	2 to 3-A:1-B
	Cartridge or stored pressure	33 gal (wheeled)	125 L	20-A
AFFF	Stored pressure	2½ gal	9.5 L	3-A:20-B
	Nitrogen cylinder	33 gal (wheeled)	125 L	20-A:160-B
Carbon dioxide	Self-expellant	2 to 5 lb	0.9 to 2.26 kg	1 to 5-B:C
	Self-expellant	10 to 15 lb	4.5 to 6.8 kg	2 to 10-B:C
	Self-expellant	20 lb	9 kg	10-B:C
	Self-expellant	50 to 100 lb (wheeled)	22.6 to 45.3 kg	10 to 20-B:C
Dry chemical (sodium bicarbonate)	Stored pressure	1 lb	0.45 kg	1 to 2-B:C
	Stored pressure	1½ to 2½ lb	0.68 to 1.13 kg	2 to 10-B:C
	Cartridge or stored pressure	2¾ to 5 lb	1.24 to 2.26 kg	5 to 20-B:C
	Cartridge or stored pressure	6 to 30 lb	2.7 to 13.6 kg	10 to 160-B:C
	Nitrogen cylinder or stored pressure	75 to 350 lb (wheeled)	34 to 158.7 kg	40 to 320-B:C
Dry chemical (potassium bicarbonate)	Stored pressure	1 to 2 lb	0.45 to 0.9 kg	1 to 5-B:C
	Cartridge or stored pressure	2¼ to 5 lb	1.02 to 2.26 kg	5 to 20-B:C
	Cartridge or stored pressure	5½ to 10 lb	2.4 to 4.5 kg	10 to 80-B:C
	Cartridge or stored pressure	16 to 30 lb	7.2 to 13.6 kg	40 to 120-B:C
	Cartridge	48 lb	21.7 kg	120-B:C
	Nitrogen cylinder or stored pressure	125 to 315 lb (wheeled)	56.7 to 142.8 kg	80 to 640-B:C

SOURCE: INTERNATIONAL FIRE SERVICE TRAINING ASSOCIATION

▼ **Table 1** *Characteristics of portable fire extinguishers (continued)*

Extinguishing agent	Method of operation	Capacity U.S.	Metric	UL or ULC classification
Dry chemical (potassium chloride)	Stored pressure	2 to 2½ lb	0.9 to 1.1 kg	5 to 10-B:C
	Stored pressure	5 to 9 lb	2.26 to 4 kg	20 to 40-B:C
	Stored pressure	10 to 20 lb	4.5 to 9 kg	40 to 60-B:C
	Stored pressure	135 lb	61.2 kp	160-B:C
Dry chemical (ammonium phosphate)	Stored pressure	1 to 5 lb	0.45 to 2.26 kg	1 to 2-A and 2 to 10-B:C
	Stored pressure or cartridge	2½ to 8½ lb	1.13 to 3.8 kg	1 to 4-A and 10 to 40-B:C
	Stored pressure or cartridge	9 to 17 lb	4 to 7.7 kg	2 to 20-A and 10 to 80-B:C
	Stored pressure or cartridge	17 to 30 lb	7.7 to 13.6 kg	3 to 20-A and 30 to 120-B:C
	Cartridge	45 lb	20.4 kg	20-A and 80-B:C
	Nitrogen cylinder or stored pressure	110 to 315 lb (wheeled)	49.9 to 142.8 kg	20 to 40-A and 60 to 320-B:C
Dry chemical (foam-compatible)	Cartridge or stored pressure	4¾ to 9 lb	2.1 to 4 kg	10 to 20-B:C
	Cartridge or stored pressure	9 to 27 lb	4 to 12.2 kg	20 to 30-B:C
	Cartridge or stored pressure	18 to 30 lb	8.2 to 13.6 kg	40 to 60-B:C
	Nitrogen cylinder or stored pressure	150 to 350 lb (wheeled)	68 to 158.7 kg	80 to 240-B:C
Dry chemical (potassium chloride)	Cartridge or stored pressure	2½ to 5 lb	1.13 to 2.26 kg	10 to 20-B:C
	Cartridge or stored pressure	9½ to 20 lb	4.3 to 9 kg	40 to 60-B:C
	Cartridge or stored pressure	19½ to 30 lb	8.8 to 13.6 kg	60 to 80-B:C
	Stored pressure	125 to 200 lb (wheeled)	56.7 to 90.7 kg	160-B:C
Dry chemical (potassium bicarbonate urea base)	Stored pressure	5 to 11 lb	2.26 to 4.98 kg	40 to 80-B:C
	Stored pressure	9 to 23 lb	4 to 10.4 kg	60 to 160-B:C
	Stored pressure	175 lb	79.3 kg	480-B:C
Bromo-trifluoromethane	Stored pressure	2½ lb	1.3 kp	2-B:C
Bromochloro-difluoromethane	Stored pressure	2 to 4 lb	0.9 to 1.8 kg	2 to 5-B:C
	Stored pressure	5½ to 9 lb	2.49 to 4 kg	1-A and 10-B:C
	Stored pressure	13 to 22 lb	5.90 to 9.97 kg	1 to 4-A and 20 to 80-B:C

SOURCE: INTERNATIONAL FIRE SERVICE TRAINING ASSOCIATION

fire departments do not carry extinguishers for Class D fires on their trucks. They rely on fire extinguishers at the facility to which they have been called. Since Class D fires are encountered primarily in machining and milling operations, some fire departments offer "on-site" training at these types of facility on a regular basis.

PROPER USE OF FIRE EXTINGUISHERS

Depending on the size of the fire, you may face a "fight-or-flight" decision. You should attempt to use an extinguisher *only* if all of the following apply:
▶ The building has been or is in the process of being evacuated.
▶ The fire department has been or is being called.
▶ The fire is small and contained.
▶ The exit is clear—that is, you can fight the fire and still get out.
▶ You can stay low and avoid smoke.
▶ The proper extinguisher is available.

Whenever possible, use the "buddy system" so that you have a partner to back you up when you are using a fire extinguisher. If you have any doubt about your personal safety or your ability to put out the fire, or if you're not sure that the extinguisher you have is the right one for the job, leave immediately and close off the area.

Once the decision to use a portable fire extinguisher has been made, you must know how to use it correctly in order to obtain maximum effectiveness. Even though extinguishers come in a wide variety of shapes and sizes, most of them operate in a similar manner. Remember the easy acronym "PASS" if you find yourself in an emergency situation and must use a fire extinguisher:

> Pull the pin.
> Aim the extinguisher.
> Squeeze the trigger handle.
> Sweep from side to side.

Proper use is essential, because the contents of a fire extinguisher empty quickly (usually less than a minute). Sweep the nozzle back and forth, aiming at the base of the fire (the fuel). Continue to watch the fire carefully even after it appears to be out—it may re-ignite! After using a fire extinguisher, make sure that you have it checked, refilled, and recharged as necessary.

Check with your local fire department to see if they provide instruction in proper fire extinguisher use. Some fire departments are willing to send representatives to your place of business for an evaluation and demonstration.

Selecting and locating fire extinguishers

▶ Fire extinguishers should be selected on the basis of the type of hazard, the degree of hazard, and the area to be protected.

▶ They should be located along normal paths of travel. They should not be obstructed from view.

▶ They should not be mounted higher—from the floor to the top of the extinguisher—than 5 ft (1.5 m) if they weigh 40 lb (18.1 kg) or less, and no higher than 3.5 ft (1.1 m) if they are heavier than 40 lb (18.1 kg).

▶ They should be placed so that the maximum travel distance between fire extinguishers does not exceed 75 ft (22.9 m) for Class A or 50 ft (15.2 m) for Class C fires. Special considerations should be given if there are extremely hazardous conditions.

▶ They should be checked regularly to ensure that they are in their designated locations, that they have not been tampered with or actuated, and that they do not exhibit corrosion or other impairments.

Inspecting fire extinguishers

All fire extinguishers should be examined at least annually by a fire extinguisher sales and service company. Inspectors are trained to determine when fire extinguishers need recharging or repairing, and when they are required to be hydrostatically tested. This type of preventive maintenance program will ensure your fire extinguishers' operability and safety.

When you arrive at a new work site, take a few minutes to acquaint yourself with the types and locations of any available fire extinguishers. As you do so, check the date on which the equipment was last inspected. Some local guidelines call for fire extinguishers to be inspected every 6 months, but by no means should this period of time be extended beyond 12 months. (Many property owners and managers require a monthly check to ensure that there are fire extinguishers at all designated locations, and that they are in working order. In some cases, portable fire extinguishers may have been moved or discharged.) If you find that the most recent inspection date on a fire extinguisher is more than a year old, it is in your best interest to report this fact to the individual responsible for such inspections. If you are faced with an emergency, it would be futile to attempt to combat a fire with an extinguisher incapable of performing its function. It is also a good idea to take a look at a fire extinguisher's pressure gauge, if it is so equipped, to make sure that the unit doesn't need recharging.

ON-THE-JOB FIRE AWARENESS

Recall the old adage that "an ounce of prevention is worth a pound of cure." The best protection against fire, by far, is fire prevention. Observe good housekeeping practices and keep the area in which you are working clean and free of combustible materials. This is especially important at new construction work sites, where you will often find scraps of paper and other trash, wood shavings, and sawdust.

Before starting installation or service work in a building, determine whether or not any type of fire suppression or alarm system is in operation. You may wish to contact the owner or property manager and discuss the best way to proceed with your repairs. If a fire alarm system is in operation, familiarize yourself with the location of the fire alarm box. Use the utmost care when working in a confined area with a fire suppression system. You have only a short time to get out in case it is triggered. When you begin work at a new site, make it a habit to find out what types of fire extinguishers (if any) are available, and note their locations.

If you become aware of a fire emergency, employ the existing fire alarm system immediately—or, in the absence of such a system, use a cell phone or the nearest telephone to summon the fire department. After sounding the alarm, you may return to the scene of the fire (only if it is safe to do so) and attempt to control its progress.

The wise service technician considers a fire extinguisher to be one of the "tools of the trade." As a safety precaution, some technicians carry portable extinguishers with them in their service trucks or vans. If you are considering the purchase of a fire extinguisher, choose a dry chemical unit capable of controlling (at least) Class B and C fires. Why? Because Class B fires often have as their sources materials that service technicians use in the performance of their work, and Class C fires can be caused by the malfunction of electrical equipment.

FIRE HAZARDS

The fire hazards most frequently associated with refrigeration and air conditioning work may be classified under several chief sources. These sources include not only refrigerants, but also solvents, fuels, construction materials, and the products being refrigerated.

Construction materials

Some of the materials used in the construction of refrigerating equipment, especially cabinets and fixtures, are flammable. Insulation materials, sawdust and shavings, and various wood or vegetable fibers all present fire dangers. Some of the binders used in insulations, such as hydrolene, pitch, tar, resins, etc., also are quite flammable and burn fiercely. Electrical insulation is

---

▶ **SAFETY TIP** ◀

How to handle flammable and combustible liquids

To demonstrate the danger of hauling gasoline in the trunk of a car, a dramatic test was conducted in which 1 gal of gasoline was ignited inside a car trunk. The resulting explosion blasted the trunk lid and a huge fireball rose about 80 ft in the air, with a force that would have killed anyone in the car.

This test illustrated an important point: Since you can't move fast enough to get away from an explosion, you'd better do what's necessary to avoid one.

Handling flammable and combustible liquids is a common occurrence on construction projects. When you're handling these liquids, do you follow proper guidelines or do you tend to ignore and underestimate the dangers? To fully understand the real dangers involved, you must know the differences between these liquids.

Compared to a *combustible* liquid, a *flammable* liquid (such as gasoline, lacquer thinner, alcohol, and some paint thinners) is much more volatile—its vapors can ignite below 100°F, even below freezing. In contrast, a combustible liquid (such as fuel oil, kerosene, or linseed oil) must exceed 100°F to release enough vapors to ignite.

(continued next page)

usually flammable, too—cotton, rubber, linen, paper, plastics, varnishes, and waxes are common ingredients of electrical insulation. Electrical insulation, especially if oil-soaked, is a frequent source of fires. When using a torch around any of these materials, first make sure that the flammable material is protected. A small piece of insulation or wood may smolder unnoticed initially, and later burst into flame.

Air conditioned spaces

Perhaps the major application of refrigeration is in the preparation and preservation of foods and beverages, which for the most part are nonflammable under normal refrigeration conditions. However, in the case of air conditioning, the spaces cooled may contain many materials that *are* flammable. Care must be exercised during installation and service, so that carpets, furniture, linoleum, draperies, clothing, and other products are not subjected to conditions (brought on by the service technician or by the equipment) that may start disastrous fires.

Oils

Lubricating oils, when in their proper containers or in the equipment itself, do not normally present fire hazards. But often, due to spilling or over-oiling, leaky seals, loose bearings, or defective oil cups and reservoirs, lubricating oils are thrown on the equipment and are ignited, thus causing a fire. Keep machines clean! This does *not* mean merely wiping off the worst of the dirt and grime. It means wiping them dry, even in places that are difficult to clean, such as finned condensers, motors, etc. If necessary, remove parts and do a good job of cleaning them. Any oily machine can be a source of fire. Cleanliness of equipment cannot be over-emphasized.

Solvents

Most of the cleaning solvents used by a service technician are flammable. Carbon tetrachloride is nonflammable, but no longer used. Petroleum spirits and other popular solvents, made by various companies under different names, may be called "high flash point naphthas," since they do not vaporize into flammable vapors until they are warmed to a temperature of 100°F (38°C) or higher. Regular naphtha gives off flammable vapors at temperatures as low as 30°F (–1°C.)

Most solvents may be handled and used with reasonable safety at ordinary room temperatures, but they are not safe at temperatures above 100°F (38°C). In all cases, keep the room well-ventilated, preferably with exhaust fans, and keep fires and sparks away from the solvents, and from their fumes. High-test naphthas, benzene, xylene, and toluene have low flash

(continued from previous page)

Whenever handling liquids in containers marked "flammable" or "combustible," be sure to read the warning label. Remember, in addition to the dangers of fire and explosion, there may be other serious health threats from these liquids, such as inhaling vapors or eye and skin contact.

Listed safety containers are required for storing, handling, and transporting flammable or combustible liquids of any quantity.

SOURCE: ACCA

points of 30°F (–1°C) and below, and are so highly flammable that they should not be used in ordinary service and maintenance work. *Never* smoke, or permit smoking by others, when handling or using any of the flammable solvents.

Fuels

Natural gas, artificial gas (manufactured gas), LP gas (butane or propane), kerosene, fuel oils of various grades, and gasoline are all fuels. Also classed as fuels are acetylene, alcohol, and other liquids used in torches. All of these are highly flammable and, if confined, explosive. They must be handled with care. Guard against spillage and accumulation of vapors from the liquid fuels, or escape of the gaseous fuels.

HOUSEKEEPING

Housekeeping, as it pertains to fire prevention and protection, includes the proper storage of material and equipment and the regular clean-up and disposal of waste and debris. Maintaining a clean and orderly workplace reduces the risk of fires. In addition to your normal housekeeping routine, observe the following practices:

▶ Waste and debris must be removed from work and traffic areas regularly (at least once a day). If it is necessary to store combustible waste materials, use a covered metal receptacle.

▶ Components of refrigeration and air conditioning systems must be kept clean in order to avoid fire hazards. Service technicians cannot work effectively and safely if components are dirty and greasy.

▶ Be aware that cleaning materials can create hazards. Combustible sweeping compounds, such as oil-treated sawdust, can be a fire hazard. Floor coverings or floor-cleaning solutions that contain low flash point materials can be dangerous. All oily mops and rags should be stored in metal containers.

▶ Make sure that fire extinguishers are accessible, properly maintained, regularly inspected, and promptly refilled after use.

PRECAUTIONS

Some of the common conditions present in *all* residences and workplaces that cause fires are:

▶ electrical malfunctions
▶ friction
▶ open flames
▶ sparks
▶ hot surfaces
▶ cigarette smoking.

Proper awareness and monitoring of these conditions can reduce fire hazards and eliminate accidents. Following are suggestions concerning precautions that you can take to reduce the risk of fire, both at home and on the job:

▶ Every service technician should keep a good fire extinguisher in his or her vehicle. It should be inspected at least once every six months to be sure that it is filled and in good working order.

▶ Every shop should have at least one fire extinguisher always available, and always in good condition.

▶ When using a fire extinguisher, direct the stream at the base of the flame, not on the flame itself.

▶ Never throw water on an oil, gasoline, naphtha, or grease fire. Water does more harm than good, and will only spread the fire.

▶ Do not leave oily rags or mops around. They often cause *spontaneous combustion* and burst into flames, frequently in an out-of-the way, unobserved place, or during the night, so that the fire gets a "head start" before it is discovered.

▶ Statistics show that three out of ten fires are caused by the careless disposal of smoldering cigarettes and matches. Remember to "chaperone" your cigarette and match—*don't let them go out alone!*

▶ Change your work clothes as soon as possible if you get them oily—they constitute a potential torch.

▶ Be careful in fighting an electrical fire, burning or smoldering insulation, or a burning motor. The stream from a hose (or from some types of fire extinguishers) is a good conductor of electricity. Make sure that you use the proper fire extinguisher, or you may receive a serious or fatal shock.

▶ *Do not smoke in bed!* Many people have burned to death thinking that it might be dangerous to someone else, but not to them.

▶ Keep your shop and truck clean, and free of accumulated "junk." Keep stock in an orderly manner and leave aisles clear in case of fire or other emergency.

▶ Gases, whether highly flammable or only moderately so, must be handled with care at all times. The service technician must be alert at all times. It takes only a fraction of a second to ignite flammable gases. After that, it is too late—and nature allows no second chances.

▶ Never discharge flammable gases in an unventilated room, or in a room in which there is a flame, either in sight or hidden, in a water heater, coffee urn, etc.

▶ If you know, or have any reason whatever to suspect, that there is any flammable gas in a room, take no chances—ventilate the room at once. Do not strike a match or carry a lighted torch, or even a cigarette, into a room in which flammable gas may be present. Do not operate an electric switch. Note especially: *do not turn a switch off*—there is more arc at

---

▶ **SAFETY TIP** ◀

Don't get burned by lack of fire safety

Whether in the office or at a job site, it's important to practice fire safety. For instance, know the location of all fire exits and fire alarms. Here are some other vital tips to prevent fires:

▷ Remove trash and debris from your work area at least once a day.

▷ Dispose of oily, greasy, or paint-soaked rags and towels in covered metal containers.

▷ Keep solvents and other flammable or combustible materials in approved, properly labeled containers and stored in a proper location.

▷ Keep sparks, flames, and excessive heat away from solvents and other combustible materials.

▷ Do not use flammable liquids or solvents such as benzene, gasoline, and paint thinner for cleaning purposes unless methods are employed for their safe use.

▷ Keep fire exits and passageways clear, and firefighting equipment ready for immediate use. Know the location of fire extinguishers nearest your work area. Practice fire drills to stay prepared.

SOURCE: MECHANICAL CONTRACTORS ASSOCIATION OF AMERICA

"break" than at "make." The electric arc, even if it is inside a switchbox, may ignite the gas (unless it is the "explosion-proof" type).

FOR FURTHER INFORMATION

Further details and technical information relating to fires and fire extinguishers may be obtained from your State Department of Labor and Industry, and from the National Fire Protection Association, online at http://www.nfpa.org/. Bulk quantities of fire extinguisher educational products are available from NFPA's Online Catalog, including the "Portable Fire Extinguishers" brochure and the "Fire Extinguishers at Work" video, part of NFPA's Safe Work™ video series. Local fire departments carry supplies of NFPA consumer brochures and booklets that provide information on selecting, using, and maintaining portable fire extinguishers. ▦

CHAPTER 12

Ladders, Scaffolds, and Lifts

LADDERS

he use of either an extension ladder or a stepladder has become a daily activity for many technicians. The proper selection, use, and care of ladders are an important part of job safety. Ladders are available in a variety of materials, including wood, aluminum, and fiberglass. They are classified according to type and rated load capacity, as shown below:

Type	Grade	Duty rating
III	Household	200 lb (91 kg)
II	Commercial	225 lb (102 kg)
I	Industrial	250 lb (113 kg)
IA	Extra heavy-duty industrial	300 lb (136 kg)

The selection of a ladder should be made by considering safety rather than initial cost.

The inspection, care, and proper use of ladders is the responsibility of the technicians who utilize them in the field. The following guidelines will assist technicians with this responsibility:

▶ All portable ladders must be equipped with non-slip bases. Rubber safety feet pivot so that they are flat on the ground and prevent slipping.

▶ Set ladders up on a firm, level surface. Use a mud sill on uncompacted soil. Make sure that both feet of the ladder are secure. If one leg sinks into soft ground, the ladder can tip sideways.

▶ Make sure that the base of the ladder is at a distance from the wall equal to ¼ of the working length of the ladder, as shown in Figure 1 (e.g., if the working length of your ladder is 16 ft, its base should be 4 ft away from the wall).

▶ Tie off or otherwise secure ladders to prevent movement. If this is not possible, one worker should hold the base of the ladder while another uses it.

▶ All ladders erected between levels must be securely fastened, extend 3 ft (90 cm) above the top landing, and afford clear access at top and bottom (see Figure 1).

▶ Unless suitable barricades have been erected, or other adequate protection has been provided, do not set up ladders in passageways, doorways, driveways, or other locations where they can be struck or bumped.

▶ Do not erect ladders on boxes, carts, tables, scaffold platforms, manlift platforms, vehicles, or garbage bins.

▶ When work must be done from an extension ladder, the ladder should be long enough for a worker to stand on a rung no higher than the fourth from the top.

▶ When working from a stepladder, never stand higher than the second step from the top.

▶ *Never* straddle the space between a ladder and another object (see Figure 2).

▶ When climbing up or down a ladder, always maintain three points of contact (two feet and one hand, or one foot and two hands) and always face the ladder.

▶ Workers must never use metal ladders or ladders with metal reinforcing when working on or near live electrical apparatus.

▶ Do not paint wooden ladders. Paint can hide defects. Finish with a clear, nonconductive preservative.

▶ Ladders with broken, bent, or missing steps, broken or bent side

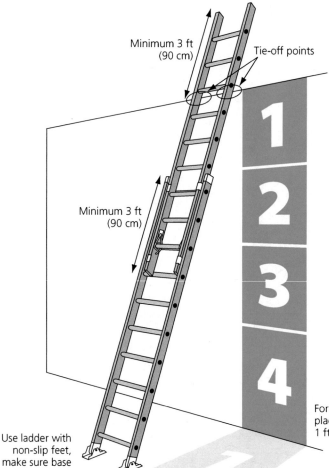

▲ **Figure 1** *Proper setup is key to ladder safety*

rails, damaged or missing bases, or other defects must not be used. They should be tagged and removed from the site.

▶ Do not use ladders horizontally as scaffold platforms, runways, or any other service for which they are not designed.

▶ Ladders transported on the top or side of vehicles should be supported and secured in proper racks to withstand braking and bumps.

▶ Ladders transported inside vehicles should be protected from damage by other equipment or material.

▶ Ladders should always be top freight—nothing should be piled on top of them.

One other commonsense caution needs to be mentioned. When a ladder is not readily convenient, fetching one often means making another trip back to the truck. *Never give in to the temptation to use some makeshift device as a way to save time. Standing on an overturned box or bucket greatly increases your risk of injury.*

Many facilities have permanent vertical ladders for access to equipment. The use and maintenance of such ladders requires special care and attention. *It is important that these types of ladders be inspected each time they are used.* A visual inspection is usually sufficient. Don't trust a vertical fixed ladder that shows signs of deterioration or damage—loose or missing bolts, excessive corrosion, cracked welds, or general lack of maintenance. Anchors, rungs, or side rails may be defective and fail under your weight. Regulations require that a vertical access ladder fixed in position must:

▶ have rest platforms at not more than 30-ft (9-m) intervals

▶ be offset at each rest platform

▶ have side rails that extend 3 ft (90 cm) above the landing

▶ have rungs that are at least 7 in. (18 cm) from the wall.

Where the ladder extends more than 16 ft (5 m) above grade or above a floor or landing, a safety cage must commence not more than 7 ft (2.2 m) above grade or above the floor or landing and continue at least 3 ft (90 cm) above the top landing with openings to permit access by a person to rest platforms or to the top landing

CONSTRUCTION SAFETY ASSOCIATION OF ONTARIO

▲ *Figure 2* *Don't take risks when working on ladders*

SCAFFOLDS

The installation of ductwork and other equipment often requires the use of a mobile scaffold. Observing the following rules will greatly ensure the safety of the user:

▶ The erection and dismantling of scaffolds must be carried out under the supervision of personnel knowledgeable and experienced in such operations.

▶ Scaffolds must be equipped with guardrails consisting of a toprail, midrail, and toeboard (see Figure 3). Guardrails must be strong enough to withstand the weight of a person leaning against them.

▶ Scaffold platforms must be at least 18 in. (46 cm) wide. A platform should be planked across its full width.

▶ Frames must be properly pinned together where scaffolds are two frames or more in height or used as rolling scaffold towers.

▶ Scaffold planks must be high-quality, defect-free, rough-sawn No. 1 spruce or better when new, and properly secured to prevent sliding.

▶ All scaffolds must be erected, used, and maintained in a plumb condition.

▶ Scaffolds must be equipped with proper ladders for access. Vertical ladders must be equipped with 6-in. (15-cm) standoff brackets. A fall protection device or safety cage is required for ladders higher than 16 ft (5 m). Use the ladder to access the work platform. *Do not climb on the scaffold framework.*

▶ Castors on rolling scaffolds must be equipped with braking devices. Castors should be securely pinned to the scaffold frame so that they cannot drop off over holes or depressions.

▶ Do not attempt to move a mobile scaffold until all personnel have dismounted and the platform has been cleared of tools, etc.

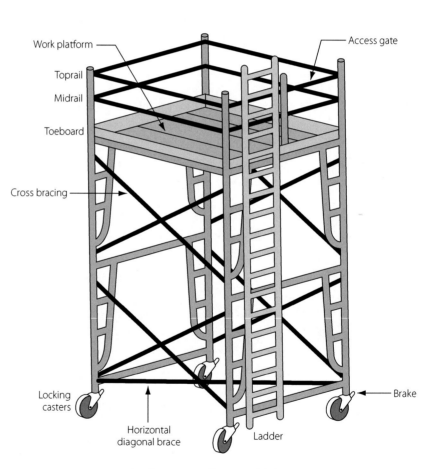

▲ *Figure 3* Rolling scaffold

▶ Maintain the proper clearance from power lines, as shown below.

Voltage	Minimum distance
Insulated lines	
Less than 300 V	3 ft (1 m)
300 V to 50 kV	10 ft (3 m)
Uninsulated lines	
Less than 50 kV	10 ft (3 m)

If it is necessary to work closer, contact your local utility company.

AERIAL LIFT DEVICES

The repair and maintenance of equipment often requires the use of an aerial lift device. These lifts are excellent temporary access tools when used properly. Such a device should be operated *only* by a worker who has been instructed in:
▶ operating the machine
▶ the daily inspections and maintenance required by the manufacturer
▶ the types of working surfaces on which the machine is designed to be used
▶ its maximum rated working load
▶ any special machine limitations
▶ the significance and location of alarms and emergency controls.
Figures 4, 5, and 6 show a variety of aerial lift devices.

Be sure to observe the following additional rules of operation:
▶ Do not use a lift that is damaged or not working properly. Have it repaired by a qualified mechanic.
▶ In the raised position, a lift should be used only on surfaces specified by the manufacturer and should never be driven close to holes, depressions, trenches, or similar hazards.
▶ A lift should not bear more than its rated working load. Where possible, the loads should be distributed over the platform.
▶ When aerial lift devices are used to lift materials, make sure that the materials are firmly secured to the platform. Avoid lifting overhanging loads.
▶ The platform or any other part of the lift should not be moved closer than 10 ft (3 m) to overhead power lines, unless the device is equipped for live

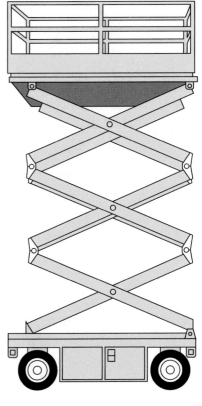

▲ *Figure 4* *Scissors lift*

electrical line work and the workers on the platform are qualified for such work.

▶ An aerial lift device should not be used for pulling, pushing, or dragging materials.

▶ Do not try to extend the platform by using planks or similar materials. Use *only* the extension devices supplied by the manufacturer.

▶ *Never* use planks or other materials to bridge the gap between the platform and the work surface.

▶ Always maintain three-point contact (two feet and one hand, or two hands and one foot) when getting on or off the lift platform.

▶ For all types of off-slab units, the terrain must be firm enough to support the machine and its rated working load.

▶ Do not use lifts under high wind conditions. This is especially important for smaller scissor lifts and boom-type machines.

▶ When the lift is not being used, turn off the power system to prevent exhaust fumes from accumulating in enclosed areas.

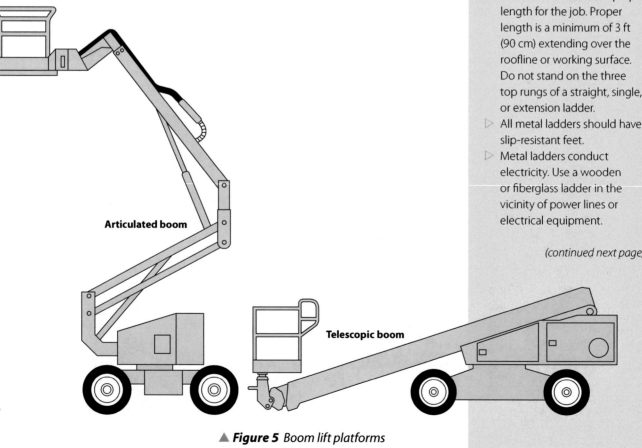

▲ *Figure 5* Boom lift platforms

Articulated boom

Telescopic boom

▶ Lifts used on ramps or on sloping or uneven surfaces must be designed for such use and properly secured against horizontal and vertical movement.

▶ On construction sites, a forklift must not be used to support, raise, or lower personnel. (In other workplaces, a forklift may be used to support, raise, or lower personnel, provided certain requirements are met.)

▶ A person working from an aerial lift device should wear a body harness with a lanyard attached to the basket or boom arm.

▶ The aerial lift boom and bucket must be properly insulated when personnel are working on any electrically powered equipment. ■

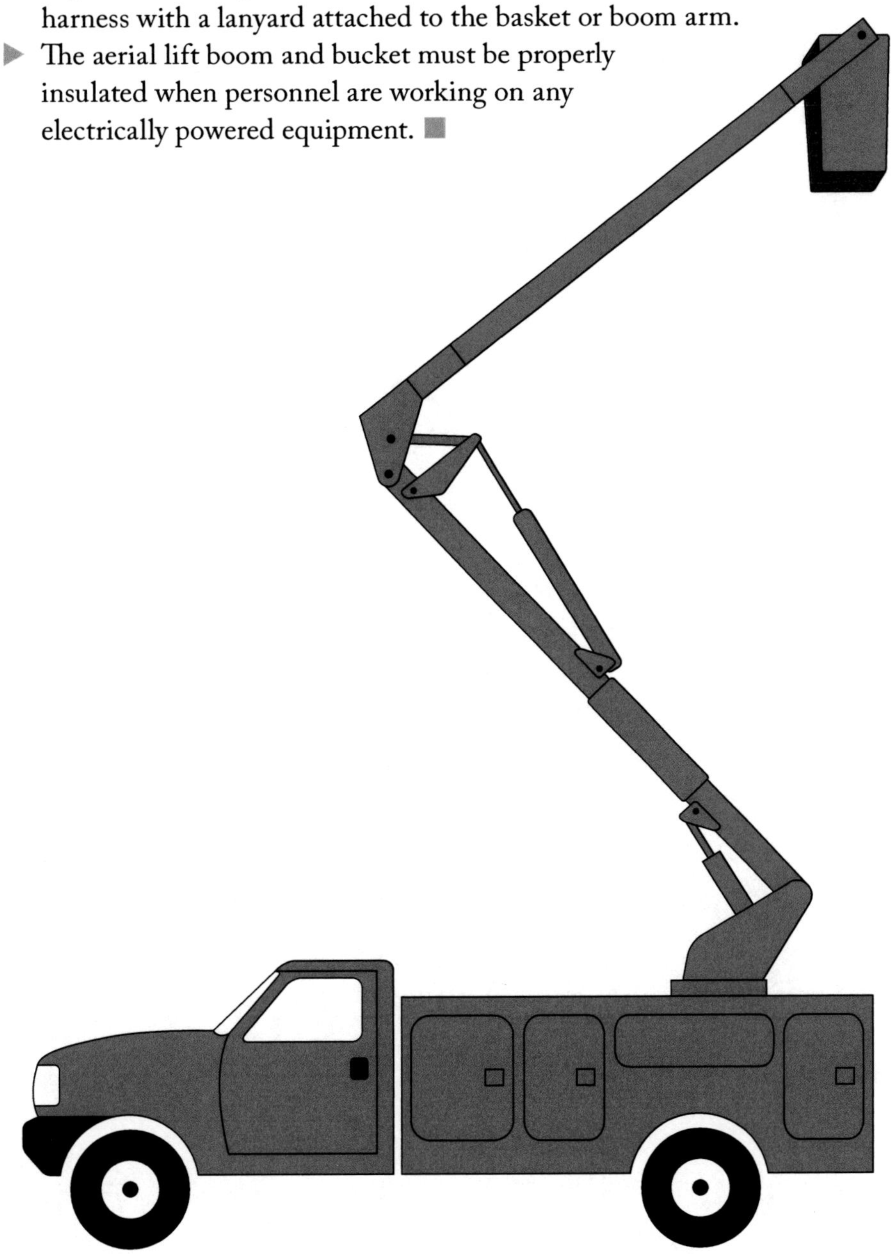

▲ **Figure 6** Bucket truck

(continued from previous page)

▷ Be sure that all locks on extension ladders are properly engaged.

▷ The ground under the ladder should be level and firm. Large flat wooden boards braced under the ladder can level a ladder on uneven or soft ground. A good practice is to have a helper hold the bottom of the ladder.

▷ Do not place a ladder in front of a door that is not locked, blocked, or guarded.

▷ Keep your body centered between the rails of the ladder at all times. Do not lean too far to the side while working.

▷ Do not use a ladder for any purpose other than that for which it is intended.

▷ Do not step on the top step or bucket shelf, or attempt to climb or stand on the rear section of a stepladder.

▷ Never leave a raised ladder unattended.

▷ Follow instruction labels on ladders.

SOURCE: U.S. CONSUMER PRODUCT SAFETY COMMISSION

Material Handling

INTRODUCTION

From the smallest bottle of chemical solution to the largest piece of equipment, material handling creates its own set of safety issues. The service technician's role in material handling will vary depending on the size and structure of the company, but nearly everyone has a hand in it at some level. It is critical for all involved to understand what is going on and what their roles are so that the job can be done safely.

CHEMICAL SAFETY

A variety of chemicals—refrigerants, oils, cleaners, adhesives—are used by HVACR technicians on a regular basis. Prior to transporting or using such products, the technician should read the label on the product, as well as the material safety data sheet (MSDS). These labels contain important information regarding the proper use of the product, safety precautions, personal protective equipment (PPE), and emergency procedures. Using chemicals the way they are intended to be used, while observing the proper precautions and wearing appropriate protective equipment, can prevent most accidents from happening. Knowing what to do in the case of an emergency *before* it happens can keep a small incident from becoming a major disaster. When reading the labels, pay particular attention to flammability, how to handle an accidental spill, and how to react to contact with the skin or eyes.

MATERIAL STORAGE

Materials need to be stored in a safe manner to help prevent accidents. Observe the following precautions:

▶ Stack materials in stable, self-supporting piles that cannot be knocked over easily.
▶ Never block aisles or exits.

▶ Keep materials that are incompatible or reactive with each other separated by a safe distance.
▶ Stack materials so that labels are visible.
▶ Keep storage areas free of materials and debris that may cause a tripping hazard or harbor pests.
▶ Store all material at least 18 in. (46 cm) below sprinkler heads.
▶ Do not manually stack or store heavy materials overhead.
▶ Keep commonly used items readily accessible.
▶ Flammable materials should be stored in a properly ventilated room that is separated from other spaces by a fire wall or fire cabinet.
▶ Gasoline and other flammable fuels should be stored in safety cans approved for flammable liquids.

MOVING MATERIALS MANUALLY

When materials must be moved manually, it is very important to consider the limitations of the human body. The human body is not nearly as easy to fix as replacing a burned-out motor or a faulty control on an air conditioning unit. A significant injury can cause years of pain or discomfort. More than 420,000 back injuries in the workplace were reported in 1999. These injuries were most often caused by bending, twisting, turning, and other motions related to improper lifting and carrying. The weight or bulkiness of the object being moved was also a contributing factor in many injuries.

When carrying material, you should use handles or holders whenever possible to improve your grip and center of balance. Always make sure that your pathway is well-lighted and free from obstacles that may create tripping hazards. Make sure that sufficient clearance exists to prevent your arms, hands, or fingers from being pinched between the load and walls or doors.

Proper PPE should be used when moving materials:
▶ gloves to protect your hands from sharp edges
▶ safety glasses to protect your eyes from debris
▶ steel-toed shoes to protect your feet from being crushed.

The most common potential injuries that can occur when materials are moved manually include the following:
▶ strains and sprains from lifting loads improperly or from carrying loads that are either too large or too heavy
▶ fractures and bruises caused by being struck by materials or by being caught in pinch points
▶ cuts and bruises caused by falling materials that have been improperly stored or have had ties or other securing devices incorrectly cut.

The high incidence of back injuries makes it impossible to overemphasize the importance of proper lifting, discussed below.

LIFTING SAFELY

The dictionary defines lifting as: "to lift, to raise in the air, to move to a different or higher position, to lift a load." Technicians find it necessary to perform this function many times during the course of their daily activities. Unfortunately, too many workers ignore the guidelines that must be followed to ensure a healthy back—it is estimated that as many as eight out of ten technicians suffer back injuries during their lifetimes. There are several risk factors known to play a role in back injuries, including:

- lack of proper exercise
- sudden twisting motions
- improper techniques used in pushing, pulling, and moving objects
- lifting and carrying loads that are too heavy
- lifting improperly.

Keeping these risk factors in mind, adhering to the following guidelines will increase your chances of avoiding a back injury.

Preventive exercises

Many people have experienced strains or sprains of the muscles, ligaments, or tendons associated with the lower back. Frequently these injuries occur while performing a simple task at home (such as picking something up or reaching for something). Similar injuries can occur while performing a task on the job.

"An ounce of prevention is worth a pound of cure," according to the old saying. Strains and sprains may be avoided by following a physical exercise program that promotes good muscle flexibility and strength. Back stretching, knee lifts, and other warm-up exercises are recommended for strengthening the back's major muscle groups. The use of a back support belt also may be required in some instances. No one wants an injury, so always consider your course of action carefully before acting. Should an injury occur, consult a doctor or other medical professional regarding the treatment required. Don't put it off—attempting to work with a bad back can aggravate the injury.

Proper lifting techniques

When an individual needs to lift, move, or carry an object, there are some basic rules to follow. Before lifting:

1. Inspect the object. Is it light or heavy? Can you grasp it properly? Think about the proper lifting techniques.

2. Inspect the area. Is the floor wet or slick? Is the area clear of debris that could cause a fall? Will the move require a twist or turn?
3. Do you feel unsure or uncomfortable about the lift? If so, get help from a coworker. When necessary, use lifting aids (dollies, handtrucks, etc.).

Proper lifting techniques *must* be employed when lifting and carrying a load. After assessing the task:

4. *Don't* bend over from the waist. Bend your knees and use your leg muscles to lift (see Figure 1).
5. Keep your back as straight as possible.
6. Do not twist your back—use your feet and legs to make a turn.
7. Move slowly and carefully.
8. Bend the knees when resetting the load.

The "robots" in Figure 2 further illustrate proper lifting techniques.

MATERIAL HANDLING EQUIPMENT

When the size, weight, or shape of the materials dictate, specialized equipment should be used to assist in moving materials. Such equipment may include carts, ropes, slings, forklifts, and cranes. It is important that you know the advantages and limitations of any type of equipment before you begin using it. All of the various types of material handling equipment have rated capacities that determine the maximum weight the equipment can handle safely and the conditions under which it can handle that weight.

◀ **Figure 1** *Wrong way and right way to lift*

Don't bend at the waist

Keep your back straight, lift with your legs

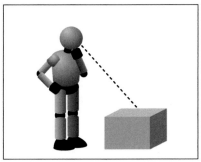

SIZE IT UP
Can you handle it or do you need help?

STAND CLOSE
Place your feet 8 to 12 in. apart

BEND YOUR KNEES
Get a good grip, keep your back straight

TIGHTEN STOMACH MUSCLES
Lift straight up, push with your legs

AVOID TURNING
Never turn or twist while lifting

USE YOUR FEET
Turn your feet to change your body position

DOWNS AND UPS
Set it down like you picked it up

HOLD ON TIGHT
Position between knee and chest level

DON'T REACH TOO FAR
Use a ladder, not a chair

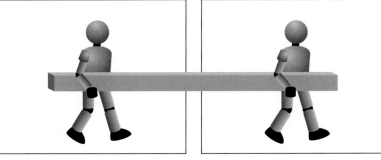

THE BUDDY SYSTEM WORKS
A little help never hurts, teamwork pays

KEEP YOUR EYES OPEN
And your field of vision clear

▲ *Figure 2* How to lift safely

Employers must ensure that the equipment's rated capacity is displayed on each piece of equipment and is not exceeded.

Hand trucks and carts

Hand trucks and carts (see Figure 3) provide a convenient way to move materials over short or long distances, thus reducing the risk of back injuries. Always make sure that the load is stable on the cart, and that the cart is not overloaded. Carts with larger pneumatic wheels should be used if the ground is not smooth. Extreme care must be taken to ensure that uneven surfaces will not cause the load to shift and become unbalanced or tip over. Always wear hand and foot protection when using a hand truck. Some hand trucks are fitted with knuckle guards, which protect the hands from being jammed into obstructions.

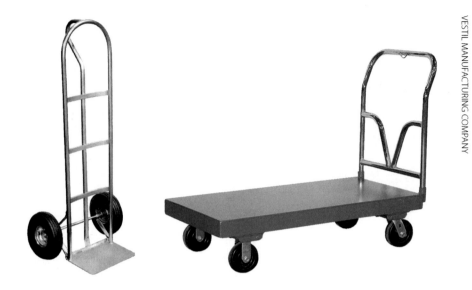

▲ **Figure 3** *Typical hand truck and platform cart*

Pallet jacks

Pallet jacks (see Figure 4) are often used to move larger loads that have been shipped or stored on skids. Always read the operating instructions and become familiar with the equipment before you attempt to move a load. Be sure to keep your hands and feet out from under the load at all times. Do not use pallet jacks on ramps. Always lower the pallet jack when it is left unattended.

Forklifts

Workers who move and store materials often use fork trucks, platform lift trucks, motorized hand trucks, and other specialized industrial trucks powered by electric motors or internal combustion engines. Employers must make sure that these workers are aware of all safety requirements pertaining to the design, maintenance, and use of such trucks. Forklifts (see Figure 5) should be driven *only* by experienced persons who have been trained in their operation.

▲ **Figure 4** *Pallet jack*

Forklifts should be equipped with overhead guards to protect the operator from falling objects. If a load becomes unbalanced or strikes some overhead obstruction, it can cause a serious injury to the person operating the equipment. *Never* place your arms or legs between the uprights of the mast or outside the running lines of the truck. Handle only stable or safely arranged loads.

Although workers may be knowledgeable about powered equipment, they should take precautions when stacking and storing material. When picking up items with a powered industrial truck, observe the following guidelines:

▶ Center the load on the forks as close to the mast as possible to minimize the potential hazard of the truck tipping or the load falling.

▶ Avoid overloading a lift truck— doing so impairs control and increases the risk of the truck tipping over.

▶ Do not place extra weight on the rear of a counterbalanced forklift to allow an overload.

▲ *Figure 5* Typical forklift

▶ Adjust the load to the lowest position when traveling.

▶ Follow the truck manufacturer's operational requirements.

▶ Pile and cross-tier all stacked loads correctly when possible.

▶ No one other than the operator should be allowed to ride on the forklift.

▶ Use seat belts.

▶ Slow down and sound the horn when crossing aisles or other areas where the view is obstructed.

▶ Forklifts should *never* be used to lift people unless a properly installed and secured personnel lift platform is used (see Figure 6).

▶ No one should be allowed to pass under the forks or under an elevated load at any time.

In the event that it becomes necessary to leave a forklift unattended, the forks should be lowered to the floor and the power shut off. If the forklift is on an incline, the wheels should be blocked. The equipment should be inspected at regular intervals for any worn or broken parts that may cause an accident.

▲ *Figure 6* Work platform for use with forklift

YALE MATERIALS HANDLING CORPORATION

VESTIL MANUFACTURING COMPANY

When materials are loaded or unloaded from trucks, trailers, or railroad cars with forklifts, provisions should be made for securing the truck, trailer, or railroad car by setting the brakes and placing chocks under the wheels. If portable dock boards are used, they should be secured in position to avoid slipping under the wheels of the forklift.

Operators must not make any modifications or additions affecting the capacity and safe operation of a truck without the manufacturer's prior written approval. Workers must not use powered industrial trucks in atmospheres containing hazardous concentrations of flammable vapors or dust.

CRANES

Employers must permit only thoroughly trained and competent workers to operate cranes. Operators should know what they are lifting and what it weighs. For example, the rated capacities of mobile cranes vary with the length of the boom and the boom radius. When a crane has a telescoping boom, a load may be safe to lift at a short boom length or a short boom radius, but may overload the crane when the boom is extended and the radius increases.

When equipment or materials are hoisted overhead, it is critical that everyone involved understands what is going to happen and what his or her responsibilities are during the lift. When all the members of the crew know where they are supposed to be and who is in charge, there is far less chance of an accident. All areas within the swing radius of the crane should be blocked off and monitored prior to and during the lift to be sure that no one is ever under the suspended load. Tag lines should be used to guide materials on or off trucks or equipment curbs. If the crane operator is operating in the blind, there should be someone to guide the operator by the use of the standard hand signals. All hoisting machinery should be marked clearly as to its lifting capacity.

RIGGING

When equipment installation or the replacement of a rooftop unit requires the use of a crane or helicopter, proper rigging is a must. Rigging of equipment or materials to be hoisted should be done *only* by experienced and trained persons. Most crane or helicopter operators and their assistants are well-qualified riggers. There may be times when a technician is asked to assist with the task. When this occurs, the rules and procedures governing the safe rigging of loads must be followed.

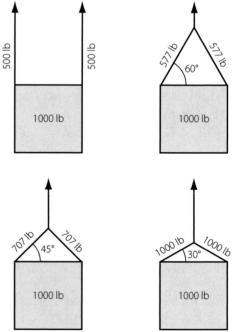

▲ *Figure 7* *Effect of sling angle on sling load*

Safe rigging depends on knowing three things:

▶ the weight of the load to be lifted
▶ the capacity of the hoisting device
▶ the safe working loads of ropes and hardware.

In addition, you should be aware of the following rigging rules:

▶ Inspect slings, hooks, shackles, and other hardware before use. Examine carefully for wear, deformity, and serviceability. Defective equipment should not merely be discarded, but destroyed to prevent inadvertent use.
▶ Rig the load with its center of gravity directly under the hook to ensure stability and avoid tipping or drifting. The load line should be vertical before the lift is made.
▶ Ensure that the sling angle is always greater than 45° from the horizontal. As you can see in Figure 7, lower angles can dramatically increase the load on each leg.
▶ Use proper hand signals to guide the crane or helicopter operator as they place the load. Figure 8 on the next page shows some of the more common hand signals for hoisting operations.
▶ Keep loads away from overhead power lines. A signal person must direct the operator of a hoisting device whenever the device or load is closer than one boom length to a power line. Observe the minimum distances shown below.

Voltage rating of power line	Minimum distance
750 to 150,000 V	10 ft (3 m)
150,001 to 250,000 V	15 ft (4.5 m)
Over 250,000 V	20 ft (6 m)

When the distance is in question, the local utility should be contacted. Utility personnel will either de-activate the line or install temporary insulation over the line.

SLINGS

Slings often are used to lift suspended loads. Slings are wrapped around the load and hooked with a hoist or crane to be lifted into place. Only persons with experience in rigging should attach the slings to the load. A load should never exceed the sling's load rating. Slings can be made of synthetic web, wire mesh, wire rope, or chain. All types of slings must be carefully inspected prior to use. Damaged slings should be removed from service

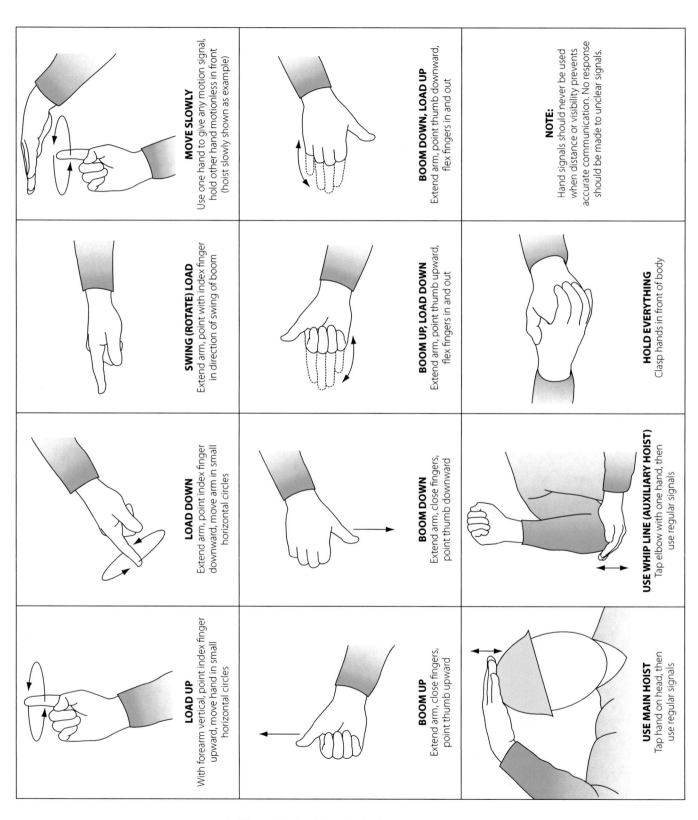

▲ **Figure 8** *Hand signals for hoisting operations*

immediately. The letters identifying the various sling configurations shown in Figure 9 are explained below:

First letter indicates	Second letter indicates top fitting	Third letter indicates lower fitting
S = single branch	O = oblong link	O = oblong link
D = double branch	S = sling hook	S = sling hook
T = triple branch	G = grab hook	G = grab hook
Q = quadruple branch	F = foundry hook	F = foundry hook

Employers must designate competent persons to conduct inspections of slings before and during use, especially when service conditions warrant. In addition, employers must ensure that workers observe the following precautions when working with slings:
- ▶ Remove damaged or defective slings from service immediately.
- ▶ Do not shorten slings with knots, bolts, or other makeshift devices.
- ▶ Do not kink sling legs.
- ▶ Do not load a sling beyond its rated capacity.
- ▶ Keep suspended loads clear of all obstructions.
- ▶ Remain clear of loads about to be lifted and suspended.
- ▶ Do not engage in shock loading.
- ▶ Avoid sudden crane acceleration and deceleration when moving suspended loads.

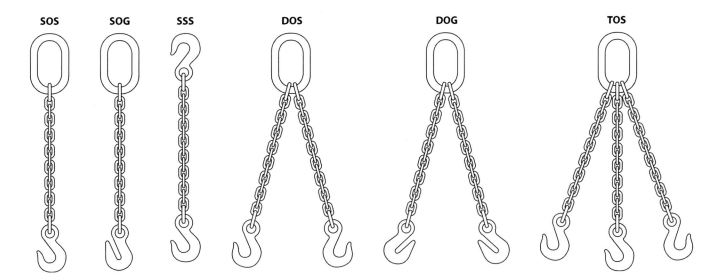

SOS SOG SSS DOS DOG TOS

▲ *Figure 9* Common chain slings

ROPE AND TACKLE BLOCKS

Ropes and tackle (see Figure 10) frequently are used for lifting tools and other smaller loads. Always wear gloves when you are working with ropes and tackle. Never let anyone stand under the load. Make sure that the ropes are strong enough for the load being lifted. (The rope should have a weight capacity of at least five time the weight of the load.) Inspect ropes for damage before use. Ropes should be protected from sharp or rough edges.

Tackle blocks can be used to reduce the amount of force required to lift a load. It is important to remember that the tackle block can lift only what the support it is hanging from can hold. Always use hooks that are rated beyond the weight of your load and be sure that the support is capable of holding the load.

Even when you are using a lifting device as simple as a rope, it is important to wear proper safety equipment. Gloves should be worn to improve your grip and protect your hands from rope burn. Safety glasses should be worn in case part of the load comes loose or you lose control of the rope. ■

▲ *Figure 10* Hand chain hoist

CHAPTER 14

First Aid

INTRODUCTION

L et's begin by defining first aid. First aid is immediate attention that is given to a sick or injured person. It may be something very simple, but sometimes a simple procedure is enough to save a person's life. It is not the purpose of this Chapter to make you a doctor or a nurse. However, it does contain some valuable information about what you can do to help someone who has been stricken with illness or injured until trained medical personnel arrive on the scene.

Properly administered first aid can save someone's life by restoring natural breathing and blood circulation, controlling bleeding, reducing the effects of shock, preventing injuries from becoming infected, and helping to conserve the victim's strength. When prompt steps are taken by someone who knows basic first aid, the injured or sick person's chances of recovery are greatly increased. An individual who administers first aid should be able to take charge, remain calm while working under pressure, and organize others to do likewise. There is no question that the first few minutes after an injury are critical. The injured person has a much better chance of full recovery if someone nearby is trained in first aid. All technicians should be able to provide basic assistance in emergency situations until proper medical attention arrives.

GENERAL PROCEDURES

No two first aid situations are exactly the same, but the following guidelines are generally applicable:

▶ If you are first person on the scene, have someone summon medical help (call 9-1-1) and instruct others to assist as necessary. If you arrive after someone else has taken charge of the situation, do as you are directed.

▶ Secure the area. Have someone remove or mark any hazards. Keep all unnecessary onlookers away from the injured parties.

▶ If several persons are injured, do your best to prioritize the injuries.

▶ Make a *primary* survey of the victim(s). This means dealing with life-threatening conditions first, and then caring for all other injuries in order of their importance.

▶ Make a *secondary* survey of the victim(s). Perform a more thorough evaluation after the obvious life-threatening injuries have been addressed.

▶ Keep the injured person lying down. Loosen restrictive clothing. Keep the victim as warm and dry as possible.

▶ Keep all wounds completely covered. Use a suitable dressing to prevent air from reaching burned surfaces. (Sometimes you may need to improvise first aid materials.)

▶ You can remove small, loose, foreign particles from wounds with a sterile gauze pad and a light brushing motion, but do not try to remove imbedded objects.

▶ Cover open fracture wounds without undue pressure before applying splints.

▶ Support and immobilize all fractures and dislocations as much as possible. Unless absolutely necessary, never move a victim until fractures have been immobilized.

▶ Test the stretcher before use. Carry the victim without rough or unnecessary movement.

Those who administer first aid must evaluate the situation with full recognition of their own capabilities and those of others on the scene. If you find yourself in this position, direct others as briefly and clearly as possible. Immediately designate someone to call for and secure professional assistance. Gathering as much information as possible on all injured persons will help medical personnel determine the extent of injuries.

PATIENT ASSESSMENT
Primary survey

Many conditions are life-threatening, but three in particular require immediate action:

▶ respiratory arrest
▶ severe bleeding
▶ circulatory failure.

Any of these conditions can set off a chain of events that will lead to death. Before caring for lesser injuries, remember to follow your "ABCs" to check for life-threatening conditions:

▶ **SAFETY TIP** ◀

First aid can be the difference between life and death

First aid is defined as immediate, temporary care given to the victim of an accident or sudden illness until the services of a physician can be obtained. Survival first aid procedures can keep an injured person breathing and control bleeding until medical help arrives.

When necessary, remove yourself and the injured person from any further threat of injury. Change the person's position only if required to administer survival first aid techniques.

Should you or one of your fellow workers require first aid, remember these safety guidelines:

1. After making sure that there is no danger to yourself and the injured person, determine the victim's level of consciousness.
2. In cases of severe bleeding, concentrate on controlling the bleeding by putting an antiseptic dressing or a clean cloth over the wound and applying direct pressure.
3. Ensure that the victim's airways are open.
4. Make sure that breathing is present and adequate. If breathing is absent, administer mouth-to-mouth resuscitation, but do not attempt first aid if you are not properly trained.

(continued next page)

A *Airways*—Establish responsiveness and position the victim to ensure adequate breathing. Artificial ventilation will be necessary if the victim is not breathing.

B *Bleeding*—Severe and uncontrolled bleeding can lead to an irreversible state of shock. Make a careful and thorough assessment to check for and control any bleeding.

C *Circulation*—In cases of circulatory failure, a person trained in CPR should check for a pulse and, if none is detected, start CPR at once.

When performing the primary survey, do not move the victim any more than necessary. Rough handling and unnecessary movement can cause additional pain and may aggravate injuries.

Secondary survey

Once the life-threatening conditions have been attended to, the secondary survey should begin. This is a head-to-toe examination to check carefully for any additional, unseen injuries that can cause serious complications:

▶ **Neck.** Examine for injury, tenderness, deformity, and/or a medical identification necklace. Spine fractures may accompany head injuries, especially in the neck area. If a spinal injury is suspected, stop until the head can be stabilized. Gently feel for any abnormalities.

▶ **Head.** Gently feel for possible bone fragments or depressions in the skull. Without moving the head, gently check for blood in the hair, scalp lacerations, and contusions. Loss of fluid or bleeding from the ears and nose is an indication of a possible skull fracture.

▶ **Chest.** Check for cuts, impaled objects, fractures, and penetrating (sucking) wounds by watching chest movement. When the left and right sides of the chest are not rising together or one side is not moving at all, there is the possibility of lung or rib damage.

▶ **Abdomen.** Gently feel the abdominal area for cuts, penetrations, and impaled objects. Look for spasms or tenderness.

▶ **Pelvis.** Check for grating, tenderness, bony protrusions, and depressions in the pelvic area.

▶ **Genital region.** Check for any obvious injury.

▶ **Upper and lower extremities.** Check for deformities, tenderness, swelling, and discoloration, which are sometimes present with fractures or dislocations. Paralysis in the arms or legs is a good indication of a fractured neck. Paralysis in the legs indicates a fractured back. Check for a medical ID bracelet.

▶ **Back.** Injuries underneath the victim are often overlooked. Look for bleeding, bony protrusions, and obvious injuries. Feel the lower back for deformity or tenderness.

(continued from previous page)

5. To help prevent an injured person from going into shock, have him or her lie down with the feet slightly elevated. Cover the person for warmth.

6. The most important thing to do for an injured person is to keep him or her quiet, protected, and reassured that everything is being done as quickly as possible.

Above all, remember that the best aid is safe work practices that eliminate injuries at the work site *before* they happen.

SourCE: MEChAnICAl ConTr ACTorS ASSoCIATIon o F AMErICA

If the victim is conscious, explain what you are doing in a calm voice. Be reassuring at all times.

In addition to being trained in first aid, you should always know what first aid equipment is available, whether you are at home, at work, or in the car. Acquaint yourself with the location of first aid supplies at each job site. Remember that first aid equipment must be checked and maintained periodically.

CAUSES OF RESPIRATORY ARREST

Breathing may stop as a result of a variety of serious accidents. The most common include overdoses of narcotics, head injuries, poisonous gases, suffocation, drowning, electric shock, and heart problems.

Poisonous gases

Several noxious gases or toxic gases found in everyday life can cause asphyxiation, including carbon monoxide, sulfur dioxide, oxides of nitrogen, ammonia, and hydrogen cyanide. Service technicians must be aware of the presence of gases in areas where they are working, and should be familiar with the warning signs. Headaches, nausea, and tearing of the eyes are among the most common. Rescuers need to protect themselves, so unless the surrounding air is good, move the victim to fresh air and begin artificial ventilation at once. Remember that some nontoxic gases (such as carbon dioxide and methane) and refrigerants may cause suffocation by displacing the oxygen in the air.

Suffocation

Get to the victim as soon as it is safely possible. Symptoms of suffocation include unconsciousness and a rapid, weak pulse. Lips, fingernails, and ear lobes become blue or dark in color. Pupils become dilated. Remember to make sure that the airway is open—artificial ventilation is of no value if the airway is obstructed.

Drowning

Get the victim out of the water as quickly as possible and begin artificial ventilation immediately. Do not waste time trying to remove the water from the victim. Drowning is a form of suffocation. The air has been cut off completely from the lungs by water or by a spasm of the larynx. This cutoff does not create an immediate need for oxygen—there is a small reserve in the lungs and tissue that can sustain life for up to six minutes or longer at low temperatures. Because this reserve is exhausted relatively quickly, it is important to start artificial ventilation as soon as possible.

Electric shock

The first thing you need to confirm is that the victim is free of the electric current. If not, that should be your first concern. Failure to do so could make you the next victim. Symptoms of electric shock are a sudden loss of consciousness, erratic breathing, and a weak pulse. Shock sometimes may cause burns as well. Breathing may be so weak or shallow that it is not detectable. Once you are sure that the person is free of the current, begin artificial ventilation or CPR.

PRINCIPLES OF ARTIFICIAL VENTILATION

Artificial ventilation is the process of forcing air to flow in and out of the lungs when natural breathing has ceased or when it is irregular or insufficient. At the top of the windpipe is a flap called the *epiglottis*, which closes over the windpipe during swallowing to keep food or liquid from entering it. When a person is unconscious, the flap may fail to respond—therefore, no solids or liquids should be given by mouth, since they could enter the lungs and cause suffocation. If an unconscious person is lying on his or her back, you must be certain that the tongue does not have the windpipe or throat blocked. If it does, the head-tilt/chin-lift maneuver should be used to open the airway. (Note that this procedure, described below, is not recommended for a person with neck or spinal injuries.) The general rules for artificial ventilation are:

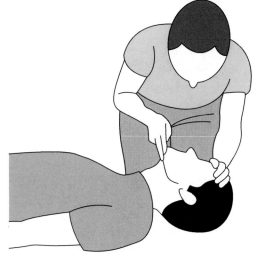

▲ *Figure 1* Head-tilt/chin-lift maneuver

▶ Do not take time to move the victim unless the accident site is hazardous. Do not delay ventilation to loosen the victim's clothing. Every second counts!

▶ Perform the head-tilt/chin-lift maneuver to open the airway and keep the tongue forward. Place one of your hands on the forehead and apply gentle, firm, backward pressure using the palm of your hand. Place the fingertips of your other hand under the chin. The fingertips are used to bring the chin forward and to support the jaw (see Figure 1).

▶ Remove any visible foreign objects from the mouth.

▶ Use a blanket, jacket, or other material to keep the victim warm and dry.

▶ Maintain a steady, constant rhythm while giving artificial ventilation and watch for chest movement (see Figure 2).

▶ Continue artificial ventilation until one of the following occurs:
  ▷ spontaneous breathing resumes
  ▷ you are relieved by a qualified person
  ▷ a doctor pronounces the victim dead
  ▷ you are exhausted and physically unable to continue.

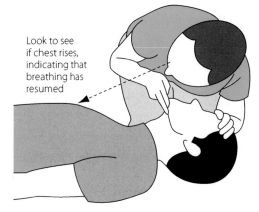

Look to see if chest rises, indicating that breathing has resumed

▲ *Figure 2* Watch for chest movement

▶ Do not fight the victim's attempts to breathe.

▶ Once the victim recovers, constant monitoring is necessary. Keep the victim lying down and treat for physical shock.

METHODS OF ARTIFICIAL VENTILATION

The first thing to do when you must treat someone who appears to be unconscious is to see if the person responds to you or not. Touch the person's shoulder and ask, "Can you hear me?" or "Are you OK?" If you receive no response, place the victim on his or her back, using the head-tilt/chin-lift method to make sure that the airway is open. Remove any loose or visible objects from the mouth. Place your ear close to the victim's mouth or nose, then:

▶ *look* for the chest to rise or fall

▶ *listen* for air escaping during exhalation

▶ *feel* for the flow of air.

If the chest does not rise and fall and no air is heard or felt, the victim is not breathing. You should begin artificial ventilation.

Mouth-to-mouth ventilation

Mouth-to-mouth ventilation is the most effective method of artificial ventilation. Follow these steps:

▶ Open the airway, remembering that the tongue is the most likely thing to be blocking the airway. Moving the jaw forward lifts the tongue away from the back of the throat and opens the airway.

▶ Kneel at the victim's side with your nearest knee next to the victim's shoulder.

▶ Use the head-tilt/chin-lift maneuver (if no spinal injury exists) to open the airway.

Pinch victim's nose closed with thumb and foreÿnger, cover victim's mouth with your own

▲ **Figure 3** *Mouth-to-mouth ventilation*

▶ Pinch the nose closed. Inhale deeply and place your mouth over the victim's mouth, as shown in Figure 3. (Instead of pinching the nose, place your mouth over both mouth *and* nose for children). Make sure that you form a tight seal. Give two full breaths into the air passage, watching for the chest to rise after each breath.

▶ Keep the victim's head extended at all times.

▶ Remove your mouth between breaths and let the victim exhale.

▶ Feel and listen for the return flow of air, and watch for the chest to fall.

If a neck injury is suspected, use a modified jaw-thrust:

▶ Place the victim on his or her back.

▶ Kneel at the top of the victim's head, resting on your elbows.

▶ Reach forward and gently place one hand on each side of the victim's chin, at the angles of the lower jaw.

▶ Push the victim's jaw forward, applying most of the pressure with your index fingers.

▶ Do not tilt or rotate the victim's head.

Repeat this procedure, giving 12 breaths per minute for adults, and 15 breaths per minute for a small child. For an infant, give gentle puffs of air from the mouth 20 times per minute.

Mouth-to-nose ventilation

In certain cases, mouth-to-nose ventilation may be required. The technique for mouth-to-nose is similar to mouth-to-mouth, except that the lips are sealed by pushing the lower jaw against the upper jaw and air is forced into the victim by way of the nose.

GASTRIC DISTENTION

One problem that may occur during artificial ventilation is the accumulation of air in the victim's stomach. Called *gastric distention*, air in the stomach can cause two problems—reduction in the volume of air that enters the lungs because the diaphragm is farther forward than normal, and vomiting.

To reduce gastric distention, proceed as follows:

▶ Reposition the victim's head to provide a better airway.

▶ Limit your ventilation force and volume.

▶ If vomiting occurs, turn the victim on his or her side (if no spinal injuries are present).

▶ Do not press on the stomach unless suction equipment is available and you have been trained to use it—otherwise, material from the stomach may become lodged in the lungs.

OBSTRUCTED AIRWAY

An obstruction in the airway can cause unconsciousness and respiratory arrest. There are many objects that can partially or fully obstruct the airway, such as food, chewing gum, tobacco, or loose dentures. Meat is the most common food to cause choking.

The first step in helping a choking victim is to attempt to remove the foreign object from the victim's mouth with your fingers. With the victim lying face up, open the victim's mouth using the cross-finger technique or, if necessary, the tongue-jaw lift, and then clear the obstruction with a finger sweep.

The *cross-finger technique* is so-called because it consists of crossing your thumb under your index finger. Brace your thumb against the victim's lower teeth and your index finger against the upper teeth. Then push your thumb and finger apart to separate the jaws. The *tongue-jaw lift* forces the victim's mouth open by grasping the tongue and lower jaw and lifting.

To perform a *finger sweep*, hold the victim's jaws open with one hand and insert the index finger of your other hand down the inside of the cheek and into the throat to the base of the tongue (see Figure 4). Sweep your index finger across the back of the throat in a hooking action to dislodge the obstruction. Grasp and remove the foreign object when it comes within reach.

When the airway is completely obstructed, the victim is unable to speak, breathe, or cough, and will probably clutch at his or her neck. Some people will use the universal distress signal—a hand raised to the neck with fingers extended around the neck is one direction, the thumb in the other direction, as though trying to choke oneself. The following paragraphs describe various scenarios and ways of dealing with an obstructed airway. (These guidelines are meant for use with adults—children and infants require slightly different techniques.)

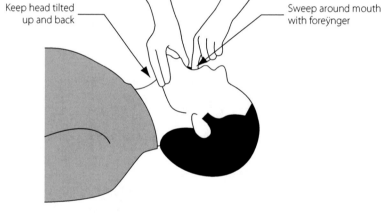

Keep head tilted up and back

Sweep around mouth with foreÿnger

▲ *Figure 4* Finger sweep

Conscious victim, sitting or standing

One method of clearing an obstructed airway is to use an *abdominal thrust* (sometimes called the "Heimlich maneuver") to exert pressure on the victim's diaphragm and dislodge the obstruction. Before administering abdominal thrusts, you first must determine if the obstruction of the airway is partial or complete. If the obstruction is partial—that is, if there is some exchange of air—encourage the victim to cough. The Heimlich maneuver should never be performed on someone who can still cough, breathe, or speak. Bend the person at the waist, head down, encourage the person to cough, and deliver a series of thumps between the shoulder blades using the flat of your palm. If applying backslaps fails to remove the obstruction, then use the following guidelines:

▶ If the obstruction is complete—if there is no exchange of air—stand behind the victim and place your arms around the victim's waist.

▶ Grasp one fist in your other hand and position the thumb side of your fist against the middle of the victim's abdomen just above the navel and below the rib cage (see Figure 5).

▶ Do not squeeze the victim. Rather, press your fist into the victim's abdominal area with a quick upper thrust.

▶ Repeat the procedure if necessary.

The *chest thrust* is another method of removing an obstruction from the airway. Use this method on a pregnant woman or on a person who is too large for you to wrap your arms around the waist:

▶ If the conscious victim is standing or sitting, position yourself behind the person and slide your arms under the armpits, so that your arms encircle the chest.

▶ Make a fist with one hand and place the thumb side of this fist on the victim's sternum.

▶ Make contact with the midline of the sternum about two or three finger-widths above the lower tip of the sternum.

▶ Grasp the fist with your other hand and press with a quick backward thrust.

▶ Repeat thrusts until the obstruction is expelled or the victim becomes unconscious.

Victim alone

It is possible to perform the Heimlich maneuver on oneself. Ball one hand into a fist and place it against your upper abdomen. Grab the fist with your other hand and make a series of upward thrusts until the airway is

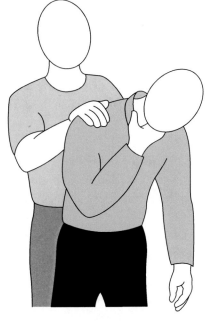

1. Stand behind the victim. Lean the person slightly forward.

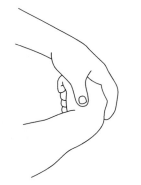

2. Make a ÿst with one hand.

3. Put your arms around the victim. Grab your ÿst with your other hand just below the rib cage.

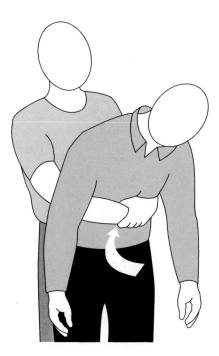

4. Make a quick, forceful movement inward and upward.

▲ *Figure 5* Heimlich maneuver

clear. If this fails, you can press your upper abdomen against a fixed object (such as leaning over the back of a chair) and repeatedly exert downward pressure until you expel the obstruction.

Unconscious victim, lying down

If the victim becomes unconscious, have someone call 9-1-1, then carefully lower the victim to the ground, making sure that the head does not hit anything. Once the victim is lying on his or her back, open the airway and look in the mouth. If you see an obstruction, try to remove it by doing a finger sweep. If you cannot see the obstruction, do *not* attempt a finger sweep—doing so may push the object farther in. After checking for visible obstructions, try to give one rescue breath. If the chest rises and falls, continue with another one. If it does not, reposition the airway, look in the mouth, and try again. If it still doesn't work, immediately start chest compressions as described below:

▶ Kneel close to or astride the victim.
▶ Place the heel of one hand on the lower half of the breast bone with the fingers elevated. The heel of the hand must be parallel to the breast bone. Place your other hand on top of and parallel to the first hand, as shown in Figure 6.
▶ With your shoulders directly over your hands, exert six to ten downward thrusts. Keep your elbows straight by locking them.
▶ Check the victim's mouth again and do a finger sweep.
▶ Repeat the procedure until the obstruction is cleared, or until further help arrives.

CARDIOPULMONARY RESUSCITATION (CPR)

Cardiopulmonary resuscitation (CPR) is an emergency first aid procedure used for victims of cardiac arrest. Information about CPR techniques is widely available, but CPR is a skill that requires professional instruction followed up by supervised practice to gain and maintain full competency. CPR training courses are available through the American Heart Association and the American Red Cross, and in some areas are offered by the local fire department. Service technicians are strongly encouraged to obtain CPR training. Be aware that the improper application of CPR, or the administration of CPR when

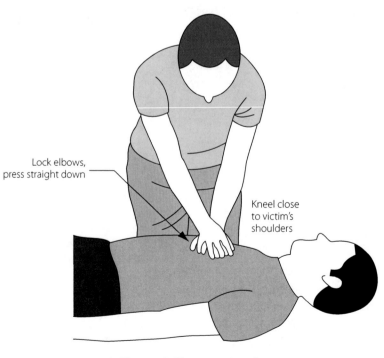

Lock elbows, press straight down

Kneel close to victim's shoulders

▲ *Figure 6* Chest compressions

it is *not* required, can result in cardiac arrest. *Never* practice these skills on another person.

BLEEDING

Bleeding (or *hemorrhaging*) is the escape of blood from an artery, vein, or capillary. Bleeding from an *artery* is characterized by bright red blood that spurts from the wound. When dark red blood flows from a wound in a steady stream, a *vein* has been cut. Blood from *capillaries* oozes slowly from the wound—there is no need for alarm, since little blood is lost this way.

There are some conditions, such as hemophilia or those caused by the side effects of some medications, that impede the clotting process. People with these conditions can bleed to death even from a slight wound. This free bleeding can occur internally as well, so you must be alert for signs of shock.

METHODS OF CONTROLLING BLEEDING

Most bleeding can be controlled relatively easily. Don't panic if the bleeding does not stop immediately—remember, blood needs time to clot. When it is necessary to control bleeding, the following methods can be used:

- direct pressure (with a sterile bandage, if available)
- elevation
- indirect pressure points
- tourniquet, if necessary (as a last resort).

Direct pressure

The best all-around method of controlling bleeding is to apply pressure directly to the wound. The is done by placing sterile gauze (or the cleanest material available) over the bleeding point and applying pressure with the hand until an outer bandage can be applied. The cover bandage knot should be directly over the wound. It should remain there until proper medical attention can be obtained. If bleeding continues, apply more pressure with another pad (do not remove the original dressing—this could disturb blood that has already clotted). If no material is available, the bare hand can be used. Any wound that cannot be controlled within a minute or two is a medical emergency.

Elevation

Elevating the bleeding part of the body above the level of the heart will slow the flow of blood and speed the clotting process. Bleeding from a hand wound, for example, can be slowed by raising the hand above the head. A leg or foot wound can be elevated above the level of the heart by helping the victim lie down flat on his or her back and propping the extremity on a chair or other object (see Figure 7). Use elevation *with* direct pressure when there are no fractures, or when fractures have been splinted and it will cause no pain or aggravation to the injury.

Indirect pressure points

In cases of severe arterial bleeding, direct pressure may not be adequate. Arterial bleeding can be controlled by applying *indirect* pressure with the finger at various pressure points. *Pressure points* are places over a bone where arteries are close to the skin. Pressing the artery against the underlying bone can control the flow of blood.

Indirect pressure must be used with caution. Once an artery is compressed over a pressure point, it must not be compressed for too long or damage to the limb can occur as a result of inadequate blood supply. (The allowable duration of pressure ranges from a few seconds to about ten minutes.) When the use of indirect pressure at a pressure point is necessary, do not substitute indirect pressure for direct pressure on the wound—use both direct pressure *and* indirect pressure. Hold the direct pressure only as long as necessary to stop the bleeding. Indirect pressure should be reapplied if bleeding recurs.

There are 26 pressure points on the body, 13 on each side, situated along main arteries (see Figure 8). If indirect pressure is necessary, you should select the pressure point nearest the wound on the side of the body where the wound is found, and between the wound and the heart.

1. The *temporal* pressure point is located next to the upper part of the ear. It is used to control arterial bleeding from the temple, scalp, or forehead. *This point can be held for very brief periods only (30 seconds maximum), since it can cut the flow of blood to the brain.*
2. The *facial* pressure point will help slow the flow of blood from a cut on the face (cheeks,

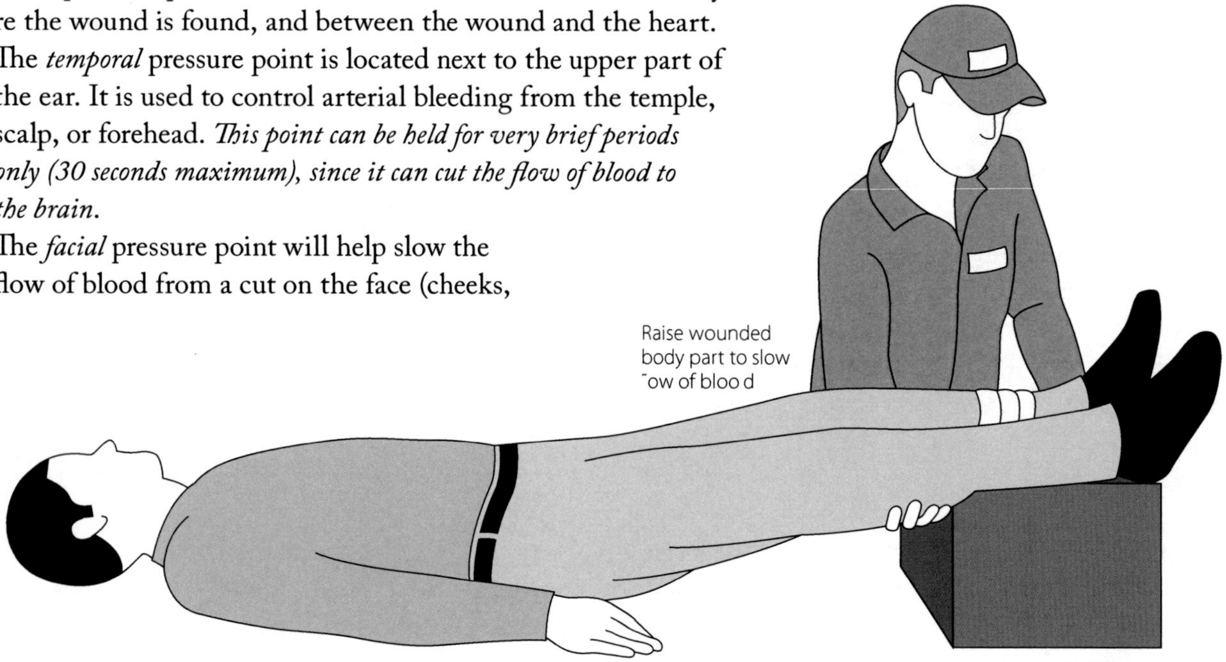

Raise wounded
body part to slow
flow of blood

▲ *Figure 7* Using elevation to control bleeding

lips, chin). It is located in the "notch" along the lower edge of the bony structure of the jaw, and should be held for a maximum of one or two minutes.

3. The *carotid* pressure points are located in the neck. *These points should be used only by experts, and must be held for only a few seconds without releasing, since they control the supply of oxygenated blood to the brain.* Do *not* attempt to use these points unless doing so is part of your training. *Never* apply pressure to both sides of the neck at the same time. There is great danger of compressing the windpipe.

4. The *subclavian* pressure point is located behind the collar bone in the "sink" of the shoulder. You must push your thumb through the thick layer of muscle at the top of the shoulder and press the artery against the collar bone. These points are used only in extreme cases, such as the amputation of an arm.

5. The *axillary* pressure point, located under the upper arm, should be pressed against the bone from underneath. It is for wounds just above the elbow.

6. The *brachial* pressure point is located in a groove on the inside of the arm near the elbow. To apply pressure, grasp the middle of the victim's arm with your thumb on the outside of the arm and fingers on the inside. Using the flat side of your fingers, not the fingertips, press the fingers toward the thumb. This is most effective for wounds in the lower arm.

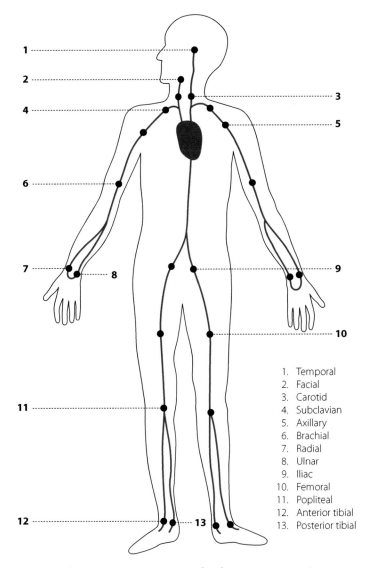

1. Temporal
2. Facial
3. Carotid
4. Subclavian
5. Axillary
6. Brachial
7. Radial
8. Ulnar
9. Iliac
10. Femoral
11. Popliteal
12. Anterior tibial
13. Posterior tibial

▲ *Figure 8* Main arteries and indirect pressure points

7. The *radial* pressure point is located on the forearm close to the wrist. It is on the thumb side of the hand, and may be held for controlling bleeding at the wrist.

8. The *ulnar* pressure point is located on the little finger side of the wrist. It can be held simultaneously with the radial pressure point to control bleeding of the hand.

9. The *iliac* pressure points often are used to control severe bleeding from a wound on the thigh, or from the amputation of a leg. The pressure

point is located on the front center part of the crease in the groin area. This is where the artery crosses the pelvic basin on the way to the lower extremity.

10. The *femoral* pressure point is located in the upper thigh. The femoral artery is deeply buried at this point, so great pressure is needed to compress the artery against the bone.

11. The *popliteal* pressure point at the back of the knee is the most effective point for controlling bleeding from a wound on the lower leg. The artery passes close to the surface of the skin, over the large bones in the knee joint.

12. The *anterior tibial* pressure point controls bleeding of the lower foot and toes. It is found on the top of the foot, at the front of the ankle.

13. The *posterior tibial* pressure point is at the back of the ankle. The anterior and posterior tibial points can be held simultaneously by encircling the victim's ankle with the hand.

Tourniquets

Generally speaking, the use of a *tourniquet* should be reserved for medical professionals. A tourniquet is a device used to control severe bleeding. It is used as a last resort after all other methods have failed. First aid providers must thoroughly understand the dangers and limitations of its use, since it completely shuts off the blood supply to a limb. A tourniquet is required only in life-threatening situations—for example, when a large artery is severed, when a limb is partially or completely severed, or when bleeding cannot be controlled by other means. Do *not* attempt to apply a tourniquet unless you have been trained to do so. Improper application of a tourniquet by inexperienced, untrained persons may cause tissue injury or even death.

INTERNAL BLEEDING

Internal bleeding in the chest or abdomen usually results from a hard blow or from a fracture of some kind. Internal bleeding is usually not visible, but it can be very serious, even fatal. Internal bleeding may be identified by any or all of the following signs and symptoms:

▶ pain, tenderness, swelling, or discoloration in the area where the injury is suspected
▶ abdominal rigidity or muscle spasms
▶ blood vomited or coughed up, or present in the urine
▶ bleeding from body orifices
▶ dizziness (exhibiting dizziness without other symptoms, especially when moving from a lying to a standing position, may be the only early sign of internal bleeding)
▶ cool, clammy skin

- weak, rapid pulse
- shallow, rapid breathing
- thirst
- confusion or light-headedness.

Emergency care for internal bleeding is similar to treatment for shock (see below). Have the victim lie down on his or her back with the legs raised slightly, and call 9-1-1. Keep the victim from becoming chilled or overheated. Never give the victim anything by mouth.

NOSEBLEEDS

Nosebleeds are more often annoying than life-threatening. They are more common during cold weather, when heated air dries out the nasal passages. First aid for nosebleeds is simple:

- Keep the victim seated, leaning forward if possible. (Do *not* have the victim lie down or tip the head back—blood may run down the throat and induce vomiting.)
- Apply cold compresses to the victim's nose and face.
- If he or she is conscious, ask the victim to pinch the nostrils together just below the bridge of the nose for about ten minutes (have the victim breathe through the mouth).
- Release the pressure slowly. Pinch the nostrils again for another ten minutes if the bleeding continues.
- Seek medical attention if the bleeding continues after two attempts to control it, or if you suspect that the nose is broken.
- Instruct the victim not to blow his or her nose for several hours after the bleeding has stopped.

Nosebleeds that cannot be controlled through these measures may signal a more severe condition, such as high blood pressure or a fractured skull. Anyone suffering a nosebleed after an injury should be examined for possible facial fractures. Under any of these circumstances, have the victim taken to a doctor.

SHOCK

Medically, the term *shock* is used to describe the effects of inadequate circulation of blood throughout the body. Shock may result from a variety of causes, and can lead to irreversible harm. The collapse of the cardiovascular system and consequent shock may be caused by any of three conditions:

- Blood is lost.
- Vessels dilate and there is insufficient blood to fill them.
- The heart fails to act properly as a pump and circulate the blood.

Symptoms of shock

The symptoms of shock are both physical and emotional. Shock can be identified by any or all of the following signs:

▶ a dazed look
▶ cold, clammy skin
▶ paleness in light-skinned individuals, ashen or grayish color in dark-skinned individuals
▶ nausea and vomiting
▶ thirst
▶ a weak, rapid pulse
▶ shallow, irregular, labored breathing
▶ dull, lackluster eyes
▶ dilated pupils
▶ cyanosis (a bluish tinge to the skin, observable in the late stages of shock).

The most important reaction that occurs in cases of shock is a decided drop in normal blood flow. Because of this decreased blood supply, the brain does not function normally—as a result, the victim's powers of reasoning, thinking, and expression are dulled. The victim may exhibit the following symptoms:

▶ a weak and helpless feeling
▶ anxiety
▶ disorientation or confusion
▶ unconsciousness (in the late stages of shock).

Treatment for shock

Circulatory shock is a serious, sometimes life-threatening condition, but it is reversible if recognized quickly and treated effectively. The first steps are to control any external bleeding and maintain an open airway to ensure adequate breathing. Then:

▶ Keep the victim lying down, if possible. Raise and support the legs if there is no injury that will be aggravated by doing so.
▶ Loosen any tight clothing around the chest, neck, or waist in order to make breathing and circulation easier.
▶ Handle the victim as gently as possible.
▶ Keep the victim warm and dry by wrapping in blankets, coats, etc. Be sure to get these coverings *under* the body as well in order to preserve body heat. (The objective is not to add heat, but to maintain the victim's body temperature as close to normal as possible.)
▶ Do *not* let the victim eat, drink, smoke, or move unnecessarily.
▶ Keep in mind that the victim's emotional well-being is just as important as his or her physical well-being. Stay calm and be reassuring. Do not

leave the victim unattended. Keep onlookers away while awaiting medical assistance.

ANAPHYLACTIC SHOCK

Anaphylactic shock is a serious, potentially fatal condition that requires rapid treatment. It is the result of a major allergic reaction within the body. People who are allergic to certain foods, drugs, insect stings, etc., should carry emergency medical identification at all times.

Anaphylactic reactions can occur within seconds after contact with the allergenic substance. Death can result within minutes. Therefore, it is extremely important to be able to recognize the symptoms of anaphylactic shock, which include:

- itching or burning skin, sometimes accompanied with red, blotchy welts (hives)
- swelling of the tongue, face, and neck
- puffiness around the eyes
- severe difficulty in breathing
- tightening or pain in the chest
- a weak pulse
- dizziness
- convulsion and coma.

Anaphylactic shock is an emergency that requires medication to counteract the allergic reaction. If the victim carries the proper medication (usually a syringe of epinephrine), help the victim take it. Arrange for transportation to a medical facility as quickly as possible. Anaphylactic shock can be fatal in less than 15 minutes. If you know what caused the reaction, notify the medical responders.

FAINTING

Fainting is a brief loss of consciousness ("black out") due to a temporary reduction in the supply of oxygen to the brain. Fainting may be caused by emotional upset, exhaustion, heat, a lack of food or fluid, or it may be a reaction to pain or fright. It may even be caused by standing up quickly after a prolonged period of inactivity. The symptoms of fainting may include any or all of the following:

- a feeling of weakness or dizziness
- dimmed or blurry vision
- pale, cold skin
- cold perspiration on the forehead
- a slowed pulse.

If a person feels faint, the initial response is usually sitting down with the head between the knees. If possible, have the victim lie down and elevate the feet (see Figure 9). Make sure that there is plenty of fresh air—open a window if necessary. Recovery from fainting is usually relatively quick and complete. If the victim is unconscious for any length of time, something may be seriously wrong. Arrange for transportation to a medical facility.

OPEN WOUNDS

An "open" wound refers to any break in the skin. The skin is the body's protective layer. An open wound not only leads to loss of blood, it also allows bacteria and germs that can cause infections to enter the body. Breaks in the skin can range from pinprick punctures to the loss of a limb. Keep in mind that an open wound may be only the surface evidence of more serious damage, such as fractures or head injuries. Open wounds are divided into various classifications. Among the most common are abrasions, incisions, lacerations, amputations, and punctures.

Abrasions

An *abrasion* is often caused by a sliding fall. The wound is seldom deep, but the top layer of skin has been scraped away and may contain dirt, gravel, or other foreign particles. Abrasions can easily become infected.

Incisions

A wound that is produced by a sharp cutting edge, like a knife or razor, is referred to as an *incision*. The edges of the wound are smooth, with no tearing or bruising. In this type of wound, large blood vessels, tendons, or nerves can be cut. Incisions bleed freely and are difficult to control.

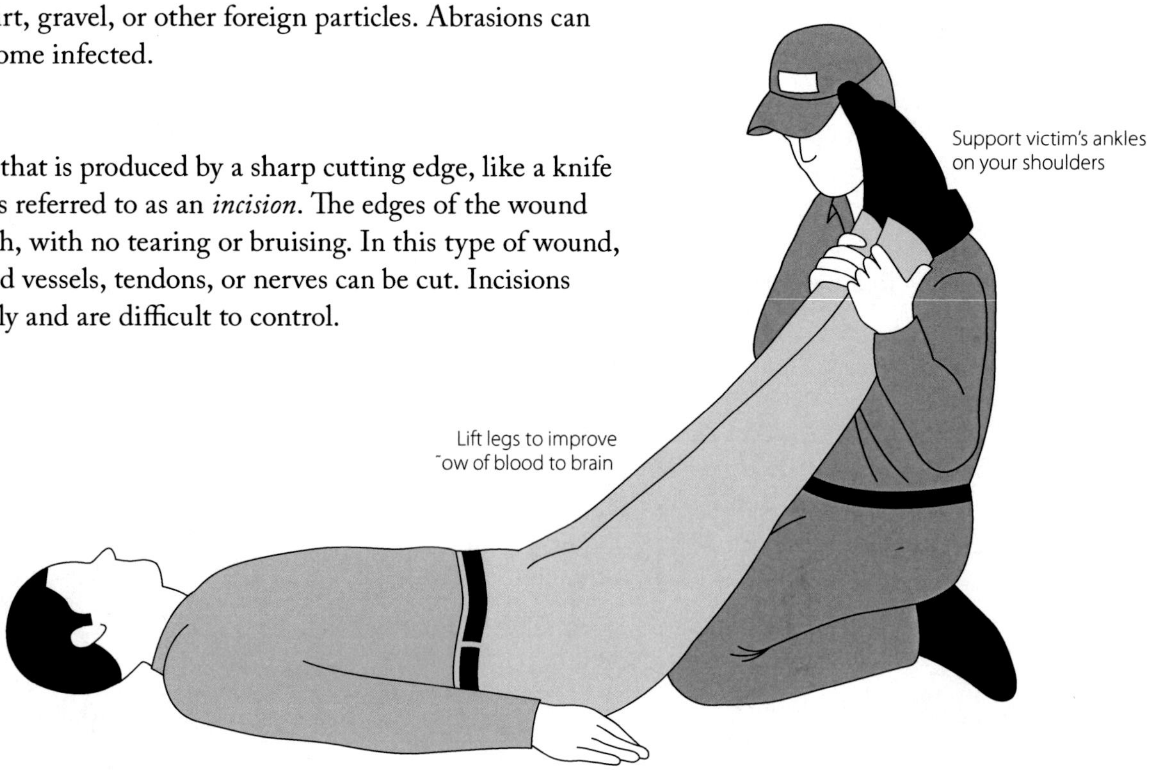

Support victim's ankles on your shoulders

Lift legs to improve flow of blood to brain

▲ *Figure 9* Recovery from fainting

Lacerations

A complex *laceration* results in rough tears and ragged edges. The flesh is torn or crushed by a blunt instrument, machinery, or jagged metal. Lacerations generally do not bleed as freely as clean-cut incisions, but there is likely to be more tissue damage. The danger of contamination and infection is high.

Amputations

An *amputation* involves the complete cutting through of an extremity (fingers, toes, hands, feet, arms, legs), leaving exposed bone. A clean-cut amputation seals off vessels and minimizes bleeding. A torn amputation usually bleeds heavily. Body parts may sometimes be successfully reattached by a surgeon.

Punctures

Puncture wounds are produced by pointed objects like needles, nails, blades, splinters of wood, or pieces of wire that pass through the skin and damage the tissue in their path. The risk of infection is high, because dirt and germs can be carried deep into the body, and because a lack of drainage may prevent free bleeding. There are two types of puncture wounds:

▶ A *penetrating* puncture, whether shallow or deep, causes injured tissues and blood vessels.

▶ A *perforating* puncture (like a gunshot wound) has an entrance wound and an exit wound. The object causing the injury passes entirely through the body, sometimes causing extensive internal damage. In many cases, the exit wound is larger and more serious than the entrance wound.

TREATING OPEN WOUNDS

When administering first aid for open wounds, your two main concerns are: 1) stop the bleeding, and 2) prevent germs from entering the wound. Keeping germs out protects against infection, which speeds up the healing process. The general procedure is:

▶ Carefully cut or tear the clothing away so that you can clearly see the injury.

▶ If loose foreign particles are present, gently wipe them away with a clean cloth or gauze. Always wipe *away* from the wound, not toward it.

▶ Do *not* try to remove any object that may be in the wound. Serious bleeding and other damage may occur if the object is removed. Stabilize the object with a bulky dressing.

▶ If possible, do *not* touch the wound with your hands.

▶ Place a sterile dressing, if available, on the wound and tape or tie it in place. Dressings should be wide enough to cover the wound and the area around it completely. If a sterile dressing is not available, use a clean cloth. Avoid fluffy material, because the fibers may stick to and contaminate the wound.

▶ If blood seeps through the dressing, do not remove it. Instead, apply another dressing on top of the first. Protect compresses or gauze dressings with a cover bandage.

▶ Keep the victim quiet and lying still. Any movement will increase circulation, which could restart the bleeding. Speak calmly and reassuringly.

▶ Treat for shock.

TYPES OF BANDAGES AND DRESSINGS

Adhesive dressings

An adhesive dressing is a self-adhering bandage frequently used for small cuts and scrapes. It consists of a pad to cover the wound and peel-off strips with a sticky backing that adheres to the skin. These common bandages come in a variety of shapes and sizes.

Bandage compresses

A bandage compress is a special dressing intended to cover an open wound. It consists of a sterile pad attached to a strip of gauze. The pads range in size from about 1 to 4 in. (2.5 to 10 cm), and usually come folded so that the pad itself can be applied directly to the open wound with no exposure to the air and without being touched by the fingers. The strip of gauze at either end of the pad can be opened and the bandage compress tied in place with no disturbance of the sterile pad. All bandage compresses and gauze dressings should be protected with a cover bandage.

Gauze

Gauze is a universal dressing used in first aid. Plain gauze can be used in place of a bandage compress to cover large wounds. It comes in various sizes and can be used in several layers. Be careful not to touch the sterile side that goes toward the wound, because this can cause infection.

Roller bandages

Roller bandages are made of gauze, cotton, or other materials. They are applied in overlapping wraps and then tied in place or secured with clips or adhesive tape. Some are form-fitting and are used to give support as well as to hold a dressing in place.

▼ **Figure 10** *Folding a cravat bandage*

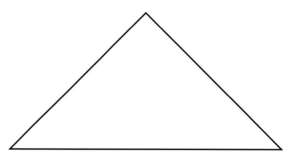
Lay triangular bandage flat on clean surface

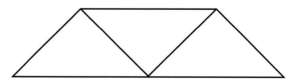
Fold triangular bandage horizontally so point touches center of base

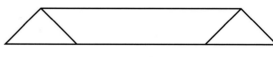
Fold in half again

Triangular bandages

A standard triangular bandage is made from a piece of clean cloth about 40 in. (102 cm) square by folding the square diagonally and cutting along the fold. A triangular bandage can be applied easily and can be handled so that the part over the wound or dressing will not be soiled. A triangular bandage also can be used to make improvised tourniquets or slings, or to apply splints.

Cravat bandages

A triangular bandage may be used open or folded. When it is folded, it is known as a *cravat* bandage. To make a cravat bandage, simply fold the cloth horizontally so that the point touches the center of the base, then fold the bandage in half again in the same direction (see Figure 10). It can be made narrower by repeating the folds. This method lets you make a bandage of the proper size to fit the situation.

Square knots

The square knot is the most frequently used knot in first aid bandaging. It lies flat, will not slip, and is easy to untie. To tie a square knot, take an end of the bandage in each hand, pass the end in the right hand over the end in the left hand and tie a single knot (as you would when starting to tie your shoelaces). Then pass the end now in the left hand over the end in the right hand, and complete the knot (see Figure 11).

The rule to remember in tying a square knot is "right over left, left over right." In order to illustrate this method more clearly, the two ends are shown in different colors in Figure 11. In reality, of course, they are two ends of the same bandage (see dotted lines).

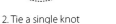

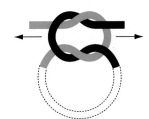

1. Right over left   2. Tie a single knot   3. Now left over right   4. Feed the left end "through the gap"   5. Pull ends ÿrmly to tighten the ÿnished knot

▲ **Figure 11** *Tying a square knot*

Slings

Slings are used to support injuries of the shoulders, arms, or ribs. In an emergency they may be improvised from belts, neckties, scarves, or similar articles. Bandages should be used whenever available.

EYE INJURIES

All eye injuries are potentially serious. Observe the following general guidelines when treating eye injuries.

Blow to the eye

▶ Hold a cold pack over the eye for 15 minutes to reduce pain and swelling, but do not exert pressure on the eye. Seek medical attention if pain persists, or if the victim's vision is affected in any way.
▶ If the victim is wearing a contact lens, do not attempt to remove it.
▶ If there is bleeding from the eye, call 9-1-1 or transport the victim to the emergency room immediately.
▶ Have the victim lie still. If a sterile pad is bandaged in place over the injured eye, cover the uninjured eye as well. This is because movement of the "good" eye causes movement of the injured one, which may damage it further.

Foreign body in the eye

▶ Do *not* attempt to remove a large object embedded in the victim's eye. Such items should be removed by a doctor, and must be protected from accidental movement until the victim receives medical attention. Stabilize the object with dressings.
▶ Again, bandage both eyes to prevent movement of the injured eye.
▶ Never leave the victim alone—many people are prone to panic when both eyes are covered. Call 9-1-1 and keep in hand contact until help arrives.

Dirt or small particle in the eye

Specks of dirt, dust, or fine pieces of metal or other substances may enter the eye and lodge there. Through an increased flow of tears, nature limits the possibility of harm by dislodging many of these small particles. If they are not removed, they can cause discomfort, inflammation, and possibly infection.

▶ Advise the victim not to rub his or her eye. Rubbing can scratch the delicate eye tissues or force the object deeper into the eye.
▶ Gently pull the upper eyelid out and down over the lower eyelid. If the particle is lodged under the upper eyelid, it is often removed in this way by the wiping action of the eyelashes as the upper eyelid returns to its normal position.

▶ If the particle remains, gently separate the eyelids and flush the eye with clean water.

▶ If the particle still remains and is visible, you may be able to lift it off with a damp swab or the corner of a piece of sterile gauze.

▶ If the particle becomes lodged in the eyeball, do not attempt to remove it. Place a bandage over both eyes. Keep the victim calm and get medical assistance.

Chemical splashed in the eye

Chemical substances, especially lime, cement, caustic soda, and acids or alkalis from storage batteries are hazardous when splashed into the eyes. The treatment is to wash eyes freely with clean water.

▶ Have the victim lie down, hold the eyelids open with the fingers, and pour the water into the inner corner of the eye from a glass, pitcher, or other clean container. Be sure to use plenty of water and wash the eye thoroughly (rinse for at least 20 minutes).

▶ Do not put neutralizing solution in the eyes.

▶ If only one eye is affected, position the victim's head so that the injured eye is lower than the other eye (to prevent water from flowing into the unaffected eye).

▶ Cover both eyes with moist sterile gauze and get the victim to medical attention immediately.

BURNS AND SCALDS
Classifications of burns

Burns may be classified according to the extent and depth of damage as follows:

▶ **First-degree burns.** The outermost layer of skin is red and tender. The skin is not broken. There may be slight swelling. This type of burn normally heals without any permanent scarring.

▶ **Second-degree burns.** The skin is swollen and red, and pain is usually significant. Blisters may form. The area may have a wet, shiny appearance if there is exposed tissue or if blisters are weeping fluid. Scarring may occur.

▶ **Third-degree burns.** All the layers of skin are burned, and the tissues, muscles, and bones underneath may be damaged. The skin has a charred, pale, leathery appearance. The victim may be insensitive to pain, due to the destruction of nerve endings. *These types of burns always require urgent medical attention.*

Burns also may be classified according to cause. The four major categories of burns are:

▶ *thermal* (both "dry," caused by flames or contact with hot objects, and "scalds," caused by steam or hot liquids)
▶ *chemical* (contact with caustic chemicals, acids, alkilis)
▶ *electrical* (lightning strikes, contact with electric current from appliances, tools, cables)
▶ *radiation* (sunburn, exposure to radioactive sources).

The seriousness of a burn or scald is influenced by the extent of the body surface involved, as well as by the depth to which the tissue has been penetrated. Cases in which a second-degree burn or scald has affected two-thirds of the victim's body surface usually result in death, but a third-degree burn over a much smaller surface area also can lead to death.

TREATMENT FOR BURNS

The first aid given to a burn victim depends largely on the cause of the burn and the degree of severity. If you are providing emergency first aid, your first priorities should be:
▶ excluding air from the burned area
▶ relieving the pain that immediately follows burns and scalds
▶ minimizing the onset of shock
▶ preventing infection.

Thermal burns

Basic care for thermal burns is as follows:
▶ Remove all clothing from the burned area, but be careful not to disturb any clothing that may be adhered to the skin. Keep the patient warm, since there is a tendency to chill.
▶ Cool the burn with clean water. Do not use ice, because it causes body heat loss.
▶ Cover the burn with a dry, sterile dressing to help prevent infection and reduce pain. Bandage loosely. Do not break blisters intentionally. Do not apply ointments or lotions to a burn unless approved by a doctor.
▶ Watch for evidence of shock and treat if it is present.
▶ Get the victim medical attention as soon as possible. In cases of severe burns, the victim will probably require an anesthetic, so nothing should be given by mouth.
▶ If the victim has thermal burns on the eyelids, apply moist, sterile gauze pads to both eyes and secure in place. Have the victim transported to a medical facility.

Chemical burns

General first aid for chemical burns is as follows:

▶ Remove all clothing containing the chemical agent. Be careful not to spread the chemical to other body parts, or to yourself.

▶ Do not use any neutralizing solution unless recommended by a physician.

▶ Irrigate with clean water for at least 15 minutes, if possible.

▶ Treat for shock.

▶ Transport the victim to a medical facility.

First aid for burns caused by contact with dry alkalis (lime, cement, fertilizers, etc.) is an exception to the general procedure for treating chemical burns, because mixing water with a dry alkali creates a corrosive substance. The dry alkali powder first should be brushed from the skin, and water then should be used in large amounts.

Electrical burns

Electrical burns can be caused by power lines, defective electrical equipment, and unprotected electrical outlets. They are treated as follows:

▶ *Make sure that the power source has been turned off or that the victim is no longer in contact with the power source before you approach the victim to provide first aid.*

▶ Conduct a primary survey of the victim. Cardiac and respiratory arrest can occur in cases of electrical burns. Be aware, too, that violent muscle contractions caused by the electricity may result in fractures.

▶ There may be two wounds—check for the points of entry and exit of the current.

▶ Cover the burned surface with a clean dressing. Do not cool the burn.

▶ Treat for physical shock and get the victim to a medical facility as quickly as possible.

▶ Respiratory failure and cardiac arrest are the major problems caused by electrical shock, not the burn itself. Monitor pulse and breathing while preparing the victim for transportation.

Radiation burns

Burns caused by solar radiation can be very painful, and may blister. Products designed specifically for sunburn usually contain aloe vera to cool the burn and reduce pain. If you are working in the sun, wear a sunscreen with an SPF of at least 15 and reapply frequently.

A rescuer who must enter a radioactive area should stay for as short a time as possible. Since radiation is undetectable by the human senses, the rescuer may receive a fatal dose of radiation without realizing it while attempting to aid the victim. Notify experts immediately of possible radioactive contamination.

SPRAINS, STRAINS, AND FRACTURES

The *musculoskeletal* system is composed of all the bones, joints, muscles, tendons, ligaments, and cartilages in the body. The makeup of the musculoskeletal system is subject to injury from sprains, strains, and fractures.

Sprains and strains

Sprains and strains are soft-tissue injuries. A *sprain* is an injury to a ligament near an ankle, wrist, or other joint. It is usually caused by a sudden twisting or wrenching movement, and results in pain and swelling, but not dislocation. Sometimes the tissues surrounding the joint are torn. A *strain* is an injury to a muscle or a tendon caused by overstretching or overexertion. A strained muscle can result in a partial tearing or pull. Symptoms of sprains and strains are similar:

▶ pain in movement
▶ swelling and tenderness
▶ sometimes discoloration.

Remember the simple "RICE" acronym for initial treatment of sprains and strains:

R *Rest* the injured area. Support and do not move the injured part.
I *Ice* the injured area. Use an ice pack or cold compress. Do not place ice in direct contact with the skin—always wrap it in a towel or other material.
C *Compress* the injured area. Use an elastic roller bandage, if available, or a thick layer of soft padding to wrap the injured extremity.
E *Elevate* the injured area. Raise and support the injured limb to reduce blood flow to the injury. A sling may be used for arm injuries.

This treatment may be sufficient. If swelling and pain persist, get the victim to a doctor. Sprains present basically the same signs as a closed fracture (see below). If you are uncertain about the severity of the injury, treat it as a fracture.

Fractures

A *fracture* is a cracked or broken bone. For first aid purposes, fractures can be divided into two classifications:

▶ In a *closed* (simple) fracture, the skin around the injured area is intact. No open wound is present, but the internal injury—the fractured bone— often causes bruising and swelling.
▶ In an *open* (compound) fracture, there is an open wound. Often part of the broken bone protrudes through the skin, causing bleeding. Exposed bone is susceptible to contamination from bacteria.

Broken bones often have sharp edges that can cut into blood vessels, nerves, or muscles. Careless or improper handling can make an injury worse, possibly converting a closed fracture into an open fracture or causing complications that greatly increase pain and shock.

For both closed and open fractures, your first aid objectives are to prevent movement, blood loss, and infection, and to arrange for the victim to be taken to the hospital.

▶ If there is an open wound, cover it with a sterile dressing and apply pressure to control the bleeding. Do *not* press down directly on a protruding bone.

▶ Secure the dressing with padding or a bandage wrapped around the limb. Bandage firmly, but not so tightly that circulation is cut off.

▶ Support and immobilize the injured limb (in an elevated position, if possible).

▶ Call 9-1-1 and treat for shock.

▶ Do *not* give the person anything to eat or drink. Do *not* attempt to move the victim unless he or she is in danger. ▪

The HVACR Training Authority

1911 Rohlwing Road, Suite A   Rolling Meadows, IL 60008-1397
Phone: 800-297-5660   Fax: 847-297-5038   www.rses.org